How To
WRITE A
THESIS
A GUIDE TO THE RESEARCH PAPER

HARRY TEITELBAUM
DEPARTMENT OF ENGLISH
HOFSTRA UNIVERSITY

MACMILLAN • USA

Third Edition

Macmillan General Reference
A Prentice Hall Macmillan Company
15 Columbus Circle
New York, NY 10023

An Arco Book

MACMILLAN is a registered trademark of Macmillan, Inc.
ARCO is a registered trademark of Prentice-Hall, Inc.

Library of Congress Cataloging-in-Publication Data

Teitelbaum, Harry.
    [How to write theses]
    How to write a thesis: a guide to the research paper / Harry
Teitelbaum.
        p.   cm.
    "Originally published by Monarch Press"—T.p. verso.
    Originally published under title: How to write theses.
    ISBN 0-671-87058-0
    1. Dissertations, Academic. 2. Report writing. I. Title.
LB2369.T36   1989
808'.02—dc19   88-37240
                                                                      CIP

Manufactured in the United States of America

10 9 8 7 6 5 4 3 2 1

CONTENTS

PREFACE

This term, you have resolved, it's going to be different. No more waiting until the long recess to sit down and write those papers due in English 28, Education 129, and Psych. 5. No more ruining vacations with endless hours spent in the library competing with all the other students who also waited until the last moment. No more scissors and paste projects, taking a little from this source and a little from that source and pasting them together with transitional paragraphs. This term you are going to approach your research papers systematically and really work, so that the paper will have some meaning for you.

This book is dedicated to help you achieve your aims. Whether this be your first or fiftieth paper, the chapters that follow will take you, step by step, from the selection and limitation of a topic to the final typed or handwritten manuscript that you will submit to your instructor. Its focus will not be on content, but rather on the mechanical aspects of preparing the paper itself. It will be a handy reference guide.

Be aware, however, that there are many different acceptable formats for a research paper. To avoid confusion, the text focuses on one form: additional forms are given in the Appendix. In the final analysis, however, it is your instructor or advisor who will determine which format he prefers, and it is this format that you will have to follow.

Since the organization and actual writing of the term paper is so closely related to that of the shorter essay, a chapter dealing with the necessary steps in writing a shorter theme —from topic selection and limitation to the writing of the final manuscript— has been added. This chapter should be of particular value to the student who has been experiencing difficulties in expressing himself coherently and clearly in written English, and for such a student it is recommended that he turn to that chapter first.

CHAPTER I

SO YOU HAVE A RESEARCH PAPER TO WRITE

The research or term paper has become so much a part of the academic scene that the student often loses sight of its primary function. Contrary to what he thinks, it is not geared to torture undergraduates and ruin their vacations nor is it a necessary evil accompanying college courses. The research paper, when carefully assigned and when conscientiously done, has definite value.

RESEARCH PAPER AND TERM PAPER: Unfortunately, these two terms have been used interchangeably all too often; they are not synonymous. Although all research papers may well be *term* papers, all term papers do not necessarily require research.

The term paper is usually a paper assigned as a major part of the course requirement. If it does not require the use of outside sources, laboratory experimentation, or questionnaire analysis, it is not a research paper. It is, then, generally a paper which may require the student to do some original thinking or evaluation. In English, for instance, it might be the close study of a text or the writing of a short story or simply a summary of some outside reading.

The research paper, on the other hand, is quite different. It requires the utilization of outside sources, laboratory experimentation, statistical analysis, and any and all other means which will enable the researcher to *search* out the solution to the problem which he has set for himself and to present this knowledge in a well-written, coherent paper to a reading audience.

REASON FOR RESEARCH PAPERS: Ideally, the research paper is supposed to make one an authority on some minute phase of an overall topic. Hence, it should incorporate an exhaustive search of any material that has been written on this given topic. Furthermore, the research should only be undertaken by the student who has already shown some interest in the subject to be researched. However, these ideals cannot always be achieved, and they often give way to one more practical. Since classroom time is limited and only so much information can be disseminated within one semester, the research paper affords the student the wonderful opportunity to become aware of different aspects of the subject under study. In a sense, it enables him to move into tangential areas, to increase his knowledge, to sharpen his insights, and, perhaps, to make new discoveries.

The research paper, then, does afford unlimited opportunities to the student—but only if approached properly. Anything that is hastily thrown together, that relies on secondary sources, that is done with the sole intent of "getting through the course" will be nothing more than an exercise in penmanship and a total waste of time.

Furthermore, the values of the research paper are, of course, not limited to the college classroom. They are an essential part of humanity's continuing desire to gain insight into and an understanding of the world. If the true purpose of higher education is to make one a better and more understanding person, then he must be given the tools with which he can continue reaching for this ideal. Whether the present college student is planning a career in medicine, science, education, or diplomacy, the ability to conduct original research will stand him in good stead. It will enable him to make important contributions to his profession, to humanity, and to himself. Research, then, is certainly one of the important tools of the educated person.

TYPES OF RESEARCH: Research generally falls into two categories, library and experimental. Although these are by no means mutually exclusive, the first type of research is one in which no experimental design is set up, where information is obtained primarily from a search of written materials. The latter is primarily a "laboratory" study.

The library-type of research requires a search of written materials. In the undergraduate paper, this search is usually limited to books and articles which can readily be found in the library. For the preparation of theses and dissertations the search will focus on primary sources and require a thorough search of *all* sources that might exist dealing with the chosen topic. Furthermore, the researcher may well have to become a sleuth, tracking down any and all leads, such as church and civil records, property transactions, personal correspondence, and even archaeological diggings.

The experimental study utilizes a somewhat different approach. To be sure, the library is still a very important aspect of this type of research since it is in the library that the researcher will be able to determine what has thus far been done on the proposed subject. Aside from this and the gathering of general background information, the experimental paper focuses more on experimentation and/or observation. The researcher must first prepare a statement of problems that he hopes to solve, and then set up an experimental design, in which he will create his control and experimental groups. This holds true whether the research is being conducted in the social or the physical sciences. Based on a careful record of his observations, he will then analyze his data, statistically if possible, and draw his conclusions.

Incorporated in the expermiental study may be the use of the questionnaire. Admittedly, there are serious drawbacks to a questionnaire study, one of these being the inability to properly validate the responses. However, where adequate and carefully selected samplings are used, where questions are constructed and phrased with utmost care, and, perhaps most important, where responses are analyzed by qualified personnel, these drawbacks may be minimized. No doubt, the advent of the computer makes the questionnaire study a more valid approach.

Again, it must be stressed that these approaches are not mutually exclusive, nor is one always better than another. That method which will enable the researcher to find the answers to the problem which he has set for himself is the best, as long as the results can be validated.

THE TOPIC: One of the major problems confronting undergraduates, and graduates too at times, is *what* to research. If it is at all possible, the student should choose a topic in which he is interested—at least one which seems to hold the promise of being beneficial to him. This is not to say, of course, that he should shy away from anything which is not in the immediate realm of his knowledge or experience. On the contrary, the research paper will offer him the opportunity to explore new areas. But there must be at least some glimmer of interest on his part, for nothing can be as dull and deadening, for both him and his reader, as spending months on a subject with which he is totally bored.

Furthermore, there must be some purpose and use for the research. Research for its own sake cannot be justified under any conditions. It seems that much that passes for research today serves no other function than to fill up pages. The research must make a definite contribution, if not to the general body of knowledge, at least to the knowledge of the researcher.

TOPIC LIMITATION: Once the topic has been selected— that is, the general area of interest that the student hopes to explore further—it must be limited so that it can be treated thoroughly and in depth. Before being able to limit, however, the student must be aware of several factors which will affect the limitation: word limitation, preparation time, library facilities, audience. Let us look at each of these individually.

The **audience**—the readers for whom the paper is being written—plays an important role in the limitation and treatment of the topic. Idealistically, the writer should not assume that the paper is being done for the sole benefit of the instructor and simply to "pass" the course. If this were the basic assumption under which he worked, the fruits of his research would be rather limited. He must know something about his potential audience: How knowledgeable are they in this field? What is their age level? Their educational level? Is the research being written for possible inclusion in a professional journal or in a lay magazine? Answers to these and other questions will certainly affect not only the topic limitation but the writer's treatment of his material. Certainly, the writer will not want to concern himself with something highly technical if his audience will consist of lay people with only a passing interest in his subject.

Perhaps even of greater importance is the **word limitation** that may have been placed by the instructor, the advisor, or a publisher. Certainly justice cannot be done to a treatment of Mark Twain's cynicism or the development of the short story in America within the confines of a 2000 to 3000 word paper. These topics would require book-length treatment. The student must remember that research demands more than a cursory, superficial treatment of a subject; the treatment must be thorough and in depth.

The **availability of material** and the **extensiveness of library facilities** are also important factors for the student to consider before limiting his topic. If he is in attendance at a small college with limited library resources, he cannot hope to undertake the same kind of research as a student at a major university—unless, of course, he is willing (and has the time and the means) to travel to those libraries where the material he seeks is available. The student in a large metropolis such as New York City has another advantage since library facilities are rather extensive. His peer, located in outlying suburbs, will generally find that local libraries are not geared for research and that, especially in comparatively new communities, periodical collections are not extensive. All these affect his topic choice.

Amount of time for the preparation and submission of the final draft is another important factor for the student to consider. All other things being equal, the student who has six months to prepare a paper is expected to do a much more intensive and extensive job than the one with six weeks. Certainly the longer the period of time to be spent in the preparation, the more wide-ranging the search can be. Here the opportunity exists for utilizing library facilities outside of the immediate area, for possible communication with potential sources, and for wider reading.

All of these factors must be taken into consideration before the student can hope to make an intelligent choice and limit his topic appropriately. However, there is another matter to be considered before this can be achieved and the library search begun. The student must have some general, overall knowledge of the broad topic he has chosen. In order to gain this knowledge, he must do some background reading. Here, a good, general source book may be of help. He should browse in the library, check the card catalog, look in the encyclopedia: any or all of these will give him some further insight into his topic.

The topic is now ready to be limited to something that can be dealt with adequately and in depth within the given restrictions. However, limitations cannot be arbitrary. There must be some valid reason for them. For example, one cannot just choose to study the short story from 1899 to 1910 unless one can justify the time limits. Nor can one choose to study Twain's pessimism in "The

Man That Corrupted Hadleyburg" and "The Mysterious Stranger" unless one can justify the choice of these two stories. Limitations cannot be haphazard and artificial.

One final word on topic limitations. Until such time as a library search has been completed, any limitation is tentative and subject to change. For one, if the student were to find a book dealing with the topic in terms of the limitations he has placed on it, he should not undertake to continue with the proposed research. For, at best, he would be presenting no more than a critical review of the text. Secondly, if his library search reveals that there is insufficient information available on his topic, it may be necessary for the topic to be broadened again. And, on the other hand, if there is too much material available to be adequately dealt with within the word limitation, then he must limit the topic even further.

Once the student has decided, based on the afore-mentioned criteria, on his limited topic and discussed it with his instructor, he is now ready to proceed with the next step in the preparation of a research paper: the library search.

CHAPTER II

THE LIBRARY

Before one can actually do any research whatsoever, he must become thoroughly familiar with the library facilities available to him. This, of course, does not include only the campus library, but the libraries in and about the community. For example, how extensive are the collections in the community library; will the student be permitted to make use of its resources; and is the local library a member of an inter-library loan association which makes material not available locally accessible to him through one of its member branches? It may well be worth some time to investigate these facilities first.

Insofar as the college library is concerned, the student should become thoroughly familiar with its organization and content before undertaking any research, since it is here, in all probability, that he will be doing the greatest portion of his work. In most colleges, a tour of the library is part of the freshman English curriculum. If, on the other hand, he is not so fortunate, he must then take it upon himself to take just such a tour.

First, he must locate various reference materials in the library: the card catalog, reserve reading room, periodical collection, general reference materials, vertical file, stacks, information desk, loan desk, special collections, computer terminals, and copying machines.

Second, the student should become aware of library hours, library rules, and regulations. For example, are undergraduates permitted to use the stacks; what is the time limit for the loan of books on reserve; are any periodicals in circulation?

Third of all, a cursory inspection of the size of the library, of the periodicals it subscribes to, of its special collection, of the friendliness of its staff, can very often give one an excellent insight into the extensiveness of the facilities and the pleasantness of the surroundings. Both of these—although the former is by far the more important—are important adjuncts to successful research.

Let us take a closer look at some of the resources that the student will be making use of.

THE CARD CATALOG: It is here that the student will probably look first since it is probably this index with which he is most familiar. Although this index might well be considered the brain of the library—it lists all the books the library owns—the student must be aware of its limitations. The card catalog lists only books and only those books which the library owns. It does not index the titles of parts of books or collections, e.g., short stories, essays, articles.

The size of the card catalog is an excellent indication of the extensiveness of the library's holdings. Hence, the size of the card catalog can readily range from one file cabinet to an entire room filled with files.

Holdings are indexed alphabetically in the card catalog; each work is catalogued under author's last name, title, and subject. Each work is classified with a **call number** so that it can be located quickly and easily. Although a thorough knowledge of the classification system is not necessary for the average student, an awareness of the method used by the library in which one works can be helpful. This is especially true where the student is permitted to go to the stacks. He will then be able to find the classes of books in which he is interested without going to the card catalog.

There are two major methods of classification currently in use: the **Dewey Decimal system** and the **Library of Congress system.** The former is used by most libraries of average size, and the latter is used by the larger libraries (including most university libraries) because of its greater flexibility.

The Dewey Decimal system divides books into ten classes, assigning each class one hundred numbers:

000–099	General Works	500–599	Pure Science
100–199	Philosophy	600–699	Technology
200–299	Religion		(Useful Arts)
300–399	Social Sciences	700–799	Fine Arts
400–499	Language	800–899	Literature
	(Philology)	900–999	History

Each main class is further divided into ten sub-divisions:

800	General Literature	850	Italian Literature
810	American Literature	860	Spanish Literature
820	English Literature	870	Latin Literature
830	German Literature	880	Greek Literature
840	French Literature	890	Minor Literature

Each of these divisions is again sub-divided into ten groups:

820	English Literature	825	English oratory
821	English poetry	826	English letters
822	English drama	827	English satire
823	English fiction	828	English miscellany
824	English essays	829	Anglo-Saxon

Further sub-divisions are indicated by decimals where each decimal unit indicates another breakdown of the general topic. To this is added a book or author number which enables the library to distinguish the many books in any one classification. The book number consists of the initial of the author's last name plus a series of numbers.

The Library of Congress system, originally devised for classifying the holdings of the Library of Congress, is a more flexible classification system and is, therefore, used by libraries which have large holdings. This system divides books into twenty main groups, assigning a letter to each:

A	General Work	L	Education
B	Philosophy—Religion	M	Music
C	History—Auxiliary Sciences	N	Fine Arts
D	Foreign History and Topography	P	Language and Literature
E	American History	Q	Science
F	American History	R	Medicine
G	Geography—Anthropology	S	Agriculture
H	Social Sciences	T	Technology
J	Political Science	U	Military Science
K	Law	V	Naval Science
		Z	Bibliography—Library Science

This system then combines additional letters and Arabic numerals for sub-divisions and to show the call number of a specific work. Since the combination of letters and numbers is almost without limit, the Library of Congress system is preferred by larger libraries.

Once the library holdings have been classified, the cards are indexed in the card catalog files. For most books there will be at least three cards: the **author** card (see page 12), the **title** card (page 13), and at least one **subject** card (page 14).

1. *ML 200.5.T5* is the number of the book. This library uses the Library of Congress classification system.

2. *Thomson, Virgil 1896* — is the name of the author and the year of his birth. In those cases where the author had died prior to the time that the card was printed, the year of birth will be followed by the year of death.

Author card:

ML 200.5
  T5   Thomson, Virgil, 1896 –
          American music since 1910. With an introd. by
       Nicolas Nabokov. New York, Holt, Rinehart and
       Winston, 1971.
          xvi, 204 p. illus., facsims., music, ports., 23 cm.
          Bibliography: p. 187 – 189.
          CONTENTS.—America's musical maturity.—American mu-
       sical traits.—The Ives case.—Ruggles.—Varese.—Aaron Cop-
       land.—Looking backward.—Cage and the collage of noises.—
       Let us now praise famous men.—The operas of Virgil Thom-
       son, by V. F. Yellin.—Music in Latin America, by G. Chase.—
       106 American composers.
            1. Music, American — History and criticism. 2. Music
          —History and criticism — 20th century. 3. Composers,
          American — Biography. I . Title.
       ML200.5.T5   780.973   SCLS 2767-25
       Library of Congress   ⌊5⌉

---

3. *American . . . 1910* is the full title of the book,
place of publication, publishing company, and year of
publication. In this instance, the work also contains an
introduction to the text. (The student should note that
the library practice of capitalizing titles differs from general practice.)

4. *xvi . . . 23 cm.* specifies that the book contains 16
introductory pages and 204 pages of text, that there are
illustrations, facsimiles, music, and portraits, and that the
book is 23 centimeters (2.54 cm. 5 1 inch) high.

5. *Bibliography: p. 187–189* indicates that the bibliography begins on page 187 and ends on page 189. (This
information can be extremely helpful when preparing
one's own working bibliography by suggesting additional
sources.)

6. *CONTENTS . . . composers* indicates the table of
contents of the book. Some cards may also contain a

quotation from the title page of the book or a brief synopsis of the highlights of the work.

7.   *1. Music . . . I. Title* specifies that this book is also listed under three subject headings: (1) *Music*, under the sub-division *American*, and under the further sub-division *History and criticism*, (2) *Music,* under the sub-division *History and criticism, 20th century*, and (3) *Composers*, under the sub-division *American, Biography*. (These subject headings will suggest other headings where the student can locate additional sources.) The book is also indexed under the title. (If the title begins with the article *a, an*, or *the*, it is then alphabetized by the word following the article.) This book, then, has five cards in the card catalog.

8.   *ML 200.5.T5* is the Library of Congress call number.

9.   *780.973* is the Dewey system call number.

10.   *SCLS 2767-25* is the order number for the card.

11.   *Library of Congress* indicates that a copy of this work is shelved in and catalogued by the Library of Congress.

12.   *5* is the printer's key.

Title card:

ML 200.5   American music since 1910
   T5   **Thomson, Virgil,** 1896 –
           American music since 1910. With an introd. by
           Nicolas Nabokov. New York . . .

With the exception of the title of the book typed above the author's name, the title card is an exact duplicate of the author card.

Subject card:

ML 200.5 MUSIC—HISTORY AND CRITICISM—20th
   T5   CENTURY
           Thomson, Virgil, 1896 –

           American music since 1910. With an introd. by
           Nicolas Nabokov. New York...

The subject card is also an exact duplicate of the author card, except that the subject heading is typed above the author's name in upper case letters.

A thorough understanding of the contents of the card catalog and a careful perusal of the card can be a valuable time saver to the student doing research. Information about whether or not the book contains a bibliography, illustrations, tables, maps, introduction, or portraits can be used to good advantage. Furthermore, the subject headings at the bottom of the card give a good clue where the student might turn for further works on his topic. The student should be aware, however, that in recent years many libraries have eliminated the card catalog file and have computerized their holdings. (The use of computer terminals is discussed later in this chapter.)

GENERAL INDEXES: The card catalog, as mentioned earlier, limits itself solely to titles of books that the library has in its collection. It does not list titles of the individual articles, essays, or short stories within the books or appearing in periodicals. These are indexed in a variety of sources. Here are some of the more common ones:

Reader's Guide to Periodical Literature, 1960 to date, published semi-monthly from September to June and monthly during July and August; bound at the end of each year in one volume. The *Reader's Guide* indexes articles appearing in approximately one hundred magazines under subject, author, and title.

Poole's Index to Periodical Literature, from 1802 through January 1, 1907. Articles appearing in American and English periodicals are indexed mainly by subject.

Essay and General Literature Index, 1900 to date, published semi-annually. Indexes, essays, and articles appearing in collections by author, title, and subject.

Short Story Index, to 1958, lists short stories appearing in collections under author, title, and subject.

Granger's Index to Poetry and Recitations indexes poems appearing in collections by author, title, subject, and first line of the poem.

In addition to these general indexes, there are a multitude of indexes for special subjects or countries. Among these are *Agricultural Index, Applied Science and Technology Index, The Art Index, Business Periodicals Index, Dramatic Index, The Education Index, Engineering Index, Index to Legal Periodicals, International Index to Periodicals, The New York Times Index, Index to One-Act Plays, Index to Speeches, Public Affairs Information Index,* and *Industrial Arts Index.*

Before using any index, the student would be wise to take a few moments to read the introductory pages of the index under consideration. Here he will find explicit instructions on how the index has been organized. Also, it must be noted that simply because a work is indexed is no indication that the library has it in its holdings. However, each library does have a card file, usually in the Periodicals Room, which lists the titles of magazines and the inclusive volumes and dates that it has. Larger libraries will list their holdings on microfiche containing titles of the periodicals and call numbers of the bound editions. These microfiches can be read through the use of a special machine that magnifies them and is relatively easy to use. Also, back issues of newspapers and frequently used periodicals may be stored on microforms (microfilm, microcard, or microfiche) to conserve space. Most libraries' periodicals holdings do not antedate their year of founding.

Current issues of magazines are usually on open shelves; past issues are bound in volumes and shelved in the stacks. In most cases, magazines and newspapers are not circulated but must be read in the library.

COMPUTER TERMINALS WITH ACCESS TO DATABASES: Many libraries, especially at universities, have computer terminals with access to various databases, making the library search much easier and faster. Here, again, it is imperative for the student first to become familiar with the databases available, the procedure to be followed, the cost for printouts, and any limitations imposed by the library. Here are some of the databases being used:

MELVYL System: The MELVYL Catalog, one of the databases used by the University of California, Irvine, provides quick and easy access to the library's holdings. It indexes UCI libraries' 1.5 million books, 19,000 periodicals, and other nonprint materials. It also lists materials at the other University of California campuses, the California State Library, the Center for Research Libraries, and through Internet, other collections nationwide.

Materials can be accessed through title, author, and subject searches. Periodicals can also be located by title. Other MELVYL Indexes include *Medline* (a current five-year index to articles in medical journals), *Current Contents* (index to current periodical literature from over 6700 periodicals), *Current Contents Table of Contents* (tables of contents for current journals), and *Mags* (index of articles from 1000 journals and magazines).

INFOTRAC: This system, used by some libraries, has various indexes that can be accessed. The *InfoTrac Magazine Index* indexes almost 500 popular magazines. The *New York Times* offers evaluations of consumer products, provides graded reviews of books, movies, hotels, etc., and tracks social and economic trends. *InfoTrac National Newspaper Index* indexes the *New York Times, Los Angeles Times, Wall Street Journal, Christian Science Monitor*, and *Washington Post. InfoTrac Academic Index* covers 500 scholarly and general interest magazines in the humanities, social sciences, and general sciences. *Pro-Quest Index* lists indexes and contains abstracts of 130 current interest periodicals including the *New York Times* and *USA Today. Social Issues Resources Series Index* contains thousands of articles about the social and general sciences from magazines, newspapers, and government documents.

There are over 250 databases and search capabilities available. Some of the other programs, such as the Educational Resources Information Center (ERIC), supply not only the bibliographic references but also copies of the documents for a fee. In addition, many libraries have access to most libraries in the United States and Canada through Inter-Library Loan and can obtain the necessary materials quickly and inexpensively.

Students are advised to familiarize themselves with the programs used in libraries. They should carefully read the material prepared by them on the proper use of computer terminals, follow the directions on the computer, and never hesitate to ask the librarian for help. (For further and more detailed information on online research, consult Alfred Grossbrenner, *How To Look It Up Online*, New York: St. Martin's, 1987.)

REFERENCE BOOKS: Just as a knowledge of the use of the card catalog and indexes is an invaluable aid in conducting research, an awareness of the reference materials available is necessary before any research can be completed. Usually the investigation of a topic begins with trying to get an overview of the broad topic. This is most readily done by reading articles in reference works.

Before beginning research one should be familiar with the types of reference works available and their basic organization. A few moments spent in the careful reading of the introductory material will familiarize the student with the work's scheme of headings, cross-references, and abbreviations. He will also learn whether the articles are signed, if the work is geared for the layman or the professional, whether it contains bibliographical listings and other references, how many volumes there are, if there is a general index volume, and if there have been any supplements. This preliminary check will also enable him to note the date of publication, which is especially important if he is researching a topic where new developments are constantly taking place. The date should indicate immediately whether the work will be of any value. Whenever the student is in doubt about the value of the reference work, he should not hesitate to check with the reference librarian.

Reference books can be categorized according to the function they serve and according to their content:

1. Encyclopedias—general and specific
2. Dictionaries and word books
3. Handbooks and yearbooks
4. Atlases
5. Books of quotations
6. Biographical dictionaries
7. Bibliographies
8. Standard works basic to any subject area sometimes also circulated.
9. Indexes—general and special

The following guides to reference books are recommended:

Sheehy, Eugene P. *Guide to Reference Books*. 10th ed. Chicago: American Library Association, 1986.

Winchell, Constance M. G*uide to Reference Books*. 9th edition. Chicago: American Library Association, 1986, with supplements.

In addition, he should check and thoroughly familiarize himself with those references which are particularly pertinent to his subject.

RESERVE BOOKS: College libraries, as a rule, have a number of books on reserve—that is, not available for general circulation. In order to assure their availability, books may be placed on reserve for the students in a particular department or for a certain instructor's class.

Books which are on reserve can readily be identified in the card catalog. The cards of these books will be "tagged" with a clip, with an insert card marked "Reserved," with a cellophane envelope marked "Reserved," or in some other manner determined by the library. When a book is placed on reserve, it is removed from the stacks. The student will generally find an index listing all the books currently on reserve in a room specially set aside for them. Reserve books may be restricted to library use only or may be placed in limited circulation, ranging from overnight to seventy-two hours. To insure their prompt return, libraries usually impose a heavy fine for overdue reserve books.

EVALUATING SOURCES: A printed source does not necessarily mean a reliable one. Nor does the inclusion of a source in a library's holdings attest to its reliability. Hence, it becomes imperative that before the student makes use of any sources in the preparation of his paper, he attempt to evaluate the reliability of his materials.

All encyclopedias are not equally reliable. Those prepared for elementary or secondary school students generally will be superficial in their presentation of the material. This is equally true of encyclopedias sold in supermarkets and discount stores. Before using any encyclopedia, the student should check the age group to which it is geared, the date of its most recent revision, and, if possible, the reliability and qualifications of its editors.

Also, although the reference works listed in Sheehy's and Winchell's texts will be reliable, the degree of reliability will vary with the researcher's purpose. Some of these sources will vary in the degree of coverage, and, therefore, although the information may be accurate, all the facts may not be included.

It will be more difficult to ascertain the reliability of the books, articles, and essays that the student selects from the various indexes. However, although only a scholar in the field can make conclusive judgments, the student can use a checklist as a guide:

1. **The author:** The author's reputation is the best criterion for judging the reliability of a source. If he is well known and respected in his field, the student can rest assured that the work has merit. But an authority, say, on military strategy is not necessarily an authority on poetry. When in doubt, the student should check the writer's qualifications in a biographical dictionary such as *Who's Who*. Very often, however, the author's qualifications are listed on the title page or in the introduction.

2. **The publisher:** The more established and well known the publisher, the less likely he will be to publish unreliable works. If the student finds that the publishing firm listed on the copyright page is not known, he should question the reliability of the text. Certainly, if no publisher is listed, or if the book has been published privately, he has every right to be skeptical.

3. **Date of publication:** The year in which the book was published is indicated on the bottom of the title page. This is especially important when researching a topic where there are constantly new developments; the more recent the date of publication, the more up-to-date the content.

This is a good time to call to the student's attention the difference between numbered printings, numbered editions, and revised editions. Of these three, a *numbered printing* indicates no changes whatsoever in the text. It simply means that the book has been reprinted, usually using the original plates. A *numbered edition* indicates some changes in the text, more in the format than in the actual content. A *revised edition* indicates changes in the content and format; the extent of the changes, however, can only be determined by a comparison of the new edition with the old, or by statements made in the preface.

4. **Periodicals:** The type of magazine in which an article appears and the audience for whom it is intended are important criteria in the evaluation of published articles. Generally, the more technical or scholarly the magazine, the more reliable the articles. This, of course, is not to say that reliable articles will not appear in the popular magazines; however, the treatment of the subject will probably be more superficial since it is geared for the general public. In the evaluation of magazine articles, the student should take into account the criteria established for authors. Unsigned articles should be evaluated carefully. Lack of an author's credit does not necessarily cast doubt on the worth of the material. There are some periodicals, especially English ones, which maintain anonymity in authorship as a matter of policy. On the other hand, unsigned articles in popular magazines should be read very critically.

5. **Content:** A cursory inspection of the book—preface, introduction, index, footnotes, bibliography, appendixes—will give some clue to its reliability. In addition, spot reading will reveal whether the writer is objective or emotional; whether he tends to substantiate his opinions and arguments with facts and with cross-references to other works; whether his tone is impartial, analytical, cynical or sarcastic.

CHAPTER III

THE WORKING BIBLIOGRAPHY

Thus far the student has done some reading in general or special reference sources to familiarize himself with his subject. Based on this, and following the procedures outlined in Chapter I, he has limited his topic accordingly. In addition, he has spent sufficient time familiarizing himself with the library resources so that from here on his research will not be hampered by strange surroundings. It is at this point that he is ready to begin making use of his knowledge of the library and begin preparing his bibliography.

REASONS FOR A WORKING BIBLIOGRAPHY: Since research implies a thorough search of all available sources on a given topic, it is imperative that the student undertake a very careful and systematic search of the available sources and keep an orderly record of his search. This search cannot be a haphazard affair. The more organized the researcher is from the start, the more time he will save by avoiding unnecessary delay and repetition.

The working bibliography is just what the name implies: the bibliography that the researcher will be working with until his final draft has been submitted and accepted. In a sense, a working bibliography is never really completed, since at any time during the general preparation and taking of notes the student might discover additional sources which he will then add to his bibliography file.

PROCEDURE: Before doing anything else, the student must supply himself with a pack of 3x5 index cards. Index cards are recommended rather than slips of paper because they will hold up better over a longer period of time and under repeated handling. In addition, he must also make a resolution that he will take his time in making entries on these cards, that the entries will be done in ink (pencil tends to smudge), and that he will not make hasty entries on matchcovers, cigarette packs, and lunchbags even though he has every intention of copying these neatly "later." Unfortunately, many of these resolutions, well-intentioned though they be, fall by the wayside.

With his topic clearly limited and with full awareness of what aspect of the topic he is focusing on, the student is now ready to begin his search. It is at this time that he will begin making practical use of many of the indexes and reference sources discussed in the previous chapter.

For each source that seems to hold promise—based on the title, on the annotation, on the comment on the card in the catalog—the student should prepare a separate bibliography card. The card should include the author's name, the title of the work, the place of publication, publisher, and date of publication; this information should always be checked against the actual title page of the book before the bibliography is finalized. The cards should also include the call number, the library in which the work has been located, and, after the work has been checked, some terse comment concerning its potential worth.

The student must be careful not to overlook any potential source of information. To be sure, a card catalog is the most popular and the most frequently used. But any research paper based solely on the works located in the card catalog is not valid research. A wealth of information can be found in periodicals, in introductions to collections and texts, and in unpublished manuscripts, most notably masters' theses and doctoral dissertations.[1]

Having compiled his working bibliography, the student probably has a sizeable file of titles which *might* contain some pertinent information on his topic. (Perhaps it should be pointed out again at this time that in all probability none of these works will deal in their entirety with his topic as he has narrowed it, for if any of them should, there would be no need for him to do research on the topic; it would have already been done.)

The student might find it helpful to organize his bibliography cards so that he may check the sources easily. All essays and articles from periodicals could be filed in one group (which could then be separated according to periodical), all general reference sources filed in another group, and all general circulation works separated according to call number. Of course, any method which the student finds least time-consuming and most helpful is the best.

The next step is to check each of these sources and make a cursory inspection of the work. Incorporated in this inspection will be an analysis of the reliability of the work (using the criteria established in the previous chapter), a check of the table of contents, index, style and tone, bibliography (which might well mean additional bib-

---

[1] Masters' theses can be found indexed in *Guide to Bibliographies of Theses, U. S. and Canada,* and doctoral dissertations in *Doctoral Dissertations Accepted by American Universities.*

Although most colleges and universities have abstracts of the doctoral dissertations indexed (usually on microfilm), the dissertation itself is somewhat harder to obtain, unless it was submitted to the university where the student is doing his own research. However, copies of the dissertations can be obtained by applying to the granting university and paying a prescribed fee.

liography cards for the working bibliography), graphs, tables, and preface. Based on this, the student will make some appropriate comment on his card concerning the work's worth. Comments may range from "no good" to "excellent bibliography" to "highly subjective"; the student should make appropriate comments that will recall his reactions for him at a later date. *He should not begin reading his sources and taking notes at this time.*

Once all sources have been checked, the cards should then be filed alphabetically by author's last name (if there is no author, by first word of the title exclusive of articles), and numbered consecutively with Arabic numerals in the upper right-hand corner. Under no circumstances should any card be destroyed or discarded at this time.

Even though a work, after the check, is totally irrelevant and has been marked "NG (no good)," the card should be retained for one very simple reason. Some months hence, while the student is embroiled in his reading and note-taking, he might come across the title of a source which seems to hold great promise. He decides to get the work, but finds that it is currently unavailable. He puts in a call for it and, after several weeks of waiting anxiously, finally gets the coveted work—only to discover that it was the same work which he had checked out some months earlier and found irrelevant. Had he retained all of his bibliography cards, however, he could have checked his file and discovered immediately that the book had no merit. This would have saved him precious time and energy.

SAMPLE BIBLIOGRAPHY CARDS: Again, the neatness and orderliness of the cards must be stressed. The student should decide on a format and use it consistently, varying it a little as possible. Here are three sample entries: full-length work, an essay from a collection, and an article from a periodical.

Book by one author:[2]

```
                                              (26)
              Schoonmaker, Alan N.
LA227.3       A Student's Survival Manual:
S35
         or, How To Get an Education
         Despite It All. New York: Harper
         and Row, 1971.
HU            good biblio. ref.
                                              (A)
```

Aside from the bibliographic information, this card contains the call number of the book, the library in which the book has been located ("HU"—Hofstra University; the student should devise his own system to identify the location of the source), a comment concerning the value of the book, a rating assigned by the student ("A" in the lower right corner, meaning excellent; here again the student should predetermine a ranking system), and the card number in the upper right corner ("26"—twenty-sixth card in the alphabetical arrangement of the bibliography cards by author's last name. This number will later be used as a reference number on the notecards to identify the source of the notes.).

---

2 The basic form of the bibliography card will remain the same for all entries; the only variation will occur in the bibliographic entry. For all possible variations in that, see Chapter IX.

Essay from a collection:

McLuhan, Marshall
"Blondie." The Art of the Essay.
2d ed. Ed. by Leslie Fiedler. New
York: Thomas Y. Crowell Company,
1969. Pp. 489-493.

Pers. lib.   Not pertinent to topic.
NG   ⑱ ⒟

The general format of the card is the same, but there
are variations in the entry. The title of the essay is placed
in quotation marks; the title of the work in which it appears is underlined (italicized), and the pages on which
the essay appears are listed. As this book is located in
the student's personal library, no call number is indicated.
Since this book is not relevant, it has been rated "D." (In
the ranking schedule established here, A=excellent source,
B=pertinent information but very limited, C=interesting
but totally subjective or of questionable reliability, D=not
pertinent.)

Article from a periodical:

Lund, T.A.
"Grammar Should Be
Groovier," Education Digest,
34: 32-34. March, 1969.

Local Lit.   Delightfully written —
some potential
⑯ ⒞

No call number is listed since periodicals do not have any. In the entry, "34:32-34," the number before the colon is the volume number; those following are the page numbers. The periodical is located in the local community library.

The student is again reminded of the importance of making all entries as indicated and making them very carefully. Although this may be more time-consuming at the moment, it will save untold hours later on. Such information as the call number and the library where the source is located, plus legibility and neatness, will preclude the necessity of checking the card catalog or other indexes again. With all this in mind, the student should be able to prepare a working bibliography which will be a constant aid to him in his research.

CHAPTER IV

NOTE-TAKING

With the completion of the working bibliography the bulk of the time-consuming library work has been completed. The student now knows what sources are available and where these sources may be located. There should be no need, for the most part, for him to make use of reference sources and indexes again. He is now ready to begin his reading and to begin taking notes.

It is at this point that the greatest temptation arises to take copious notes as the student reads a book or an article and to leave the worries about organization and the writing of the paper until later. The tendency is to supply oneself with a pad of legal-size, lined yellow paper; to write industriously on every line on both sides, usually in pencil; and, to conserve time, to make frequent use of abbreviations—making them up as one goes along. Although this seems to be the shortest and easiest way at the time, it will prove to be the most time consuming and frustrating method before one is finished. Proper research and note-taking procedure begins with a statement of thesis and a tentative outline.

STATEMENT OF THESIS: From his preliminary reading, from his examination of the sources in the preparation of his working bibliography, from discussing the topic with his instructor or advisor, and from thinking about the subject, the student should be able to formulate a statement of thesis. This statement will be the guide which will enable him to focus his plan of attack and aid him in the outlining of his paper. It is the controlling factor or the focal point around which his research will revolve. It will force him to clarify his thinking, to determine what is relevant and irrelevant in his reading. It will eliminate the tendency to take endless notes which will have no bearing on his primary objective.

The thesis statement, or the statement of the problem, must be written down after careful deliberation and polished until it finally encompasses the central idea to the student's satisfaction. Usually it is stated in the form of a problem that the researcher hopes to resolve through his research, since a thesis statement technically is a statement of the solution. In research the thesis is the anticipated result that the research will either validate or invalidate.

Assume that a student is researching the writings of Stephen Crane. After preliminary reading he may have limited the topic to "Crane as a naturalistic writer," and further limited it to "naturalism in *The Red Badge of Courage*." Since he is beginning to research his topic, he is not yet certain that the book is naturalistic. Thus his problem is to determine if there are indications of naturalistic philosophy in the work and, if so, what these are. He would then formulate his statement of thesis somewhat along these lines:

Statement of the problem: To determine what aspects of naturalism are inherent in Stephen Crane's *The Red Badge of Courage*.

Although the student's own lack of knowledge might require some careful and detailed reading on naturalism *per se*, it is not a necessary adjunct to the paper. The paper, according to the statement of thesis, will limit itself to the aspects of naturalism found in the book. This will be his guideline, one which he will have to refer to frequently in the preparation of his preliminary outline. For anything that does not contribute to proving that statement is irrelevant, regardless of how interesting it may be. Hence, references to the biography of the author, to other naturalistic writers, to the origin of the naturalistic school are all irrelevant.

Let us look at another possible topic. For his topic a student has chosen "the extrinsic factors in the interpretation of poetry." Through his preliminary reading, he may have limited his topic to "the possible effect of biography in the interpretation of selected sonnets by Elizabeth Barrett Browning." He would then formulate his statement of thesis as follows:

Statement of the problem: To determine what effect a knowledge of Elizabeth Browning's courtship with Robert Browning has on the interpretation of her sonnets.

There is, of course, nothing final about the thesis statement. It may be modified as the student becomes more deeply embroiled in his research. He may discover, for example, that the topic needs to be limited further or to be broadened.

PRELIMINARY OUTLINE: If the student's reading and note-taking are to have any direction and if he is to be able to exercise any discretion in what he does and does not write down, he must draw up some plan which will act as his blueprint. This blueprint is his preliminary outline. Perhaps it might be more appropriate to call this a preliminary "tentative" outline, for such an outline is, of course, subject to change as the student does more reading and becomes more familiar with the subject under investigation. Here again the outline is not permanent until the paper has been written. However, care exercised in the preparation of this outline will require a minimum of changes later, and the fewer changes, the less time spent in needless reading, note-taking, and revising.

Preliminary outlining is an organizational process. The student should put his thoughts down on paper with the idea that he will be reviewing this outline and eliminating items which are not pertinent. At this point, it is not imperative that he follow the formal Harvard outline format, although using it will probably help him to organize his thoughts more logically. The organization may follow a chronological, logical, or cause and effect order, to name just a few. The actual order will be determined by the subject matter.

Always keeping his statement of thesis before him, the student should list those topics that he thinks should be discussed in his paper. After listing all possible topics, he should check each one against his thesis statement, asking himself, "Will this help to prove my thesis?" If the answer is no, then that topic should be eliminated. The remaining topics should be organized in a logical order, focused on solving the problem set forth in the thesis statement. This order should incorporate major divisions —indicated with Roman numerals—and subdivisions—indicated with capital letters and Arabic numerals.

The outline for the proposed paper on Naturalism in *The Red Badge of Courage* might look something like this:

NATURALISM IN *THE RED BADGE OF COURAGE*

Preliminary Outline

Statement of thesis: To determine what aspects of naturalism are inherent in Stephen Crane's *Red Badge of Courage*.

- I. Naturalism
    - A. Brief definition
    - B. Major tenets
    - C. Relation to literature
- II. Importance of details in naturalistic writings
- III. Tone of naturalism
    - A. In philosophy
    - B. In *Red Badge*...

IV. Evidences of naturalistic thought in *Red Badge*...
    A. Animalistic behavior
    B. Survival—self-preservation
    C. Effect of heredity on behavior
    D. Effect of environment on behavior
    E. Obsession with violence

V. Theme of *Red Badge* ...

This, of course, is not the first outline that the student would have done, nor is it the last before the paper will be finally completed. Although each of the items here tends to substantiate the thesis statement and hence is pertinent, changes had to be effected to reflect greater insight gained as the reading progressed. Again, then, the preliminary outline is to be used as a guide; it is tentative; and it is continually subject to revision.

NOTECARD FORMAT: With the preliminary outline prepared, the student is now ready to begin his reading. Armed with his working bibliography, he is ready to approach his reading and note-taking in a systematic manner. Since his cards contain comments and ratings, he can be selective about which works he will read first. However, first he must know something about proper note-taking procedures.

The student should supply himself with large-size index cards —4x6 or, better yet, 5x8— which he will carry with him whenever he is about to do any reading on his topic. This is an important habit to get into. He will find that, in the long run, standard-size cards are easier to handle than either notebooks or long sheets of paper. Here again it might well require breaking the old habit of jotting down notes on whatever happens to be handy at the moment. Although this process of note-taking will again seem to be more time-consuming at the start, it will make the actual writing of the paper considerably easier since it is much simpler to refer to notecards than to sheets of paper.

Armed with his working bibliography *and* his preliminary outline, the student approaches his sources. It is the bibliography cards which determine which source he reads, but it is his preliminary outline which determines what he will read in the source, and, more important, what he will write down. He should take his notes not by book, but in accordance with his preliminary outline. That is to say, from one source he might conceivably have as many cards as there are topics in his outline.

As he reads and comes to some relevant information on one of the topics from his outline, he will take a card and enter the following: on the top line, the pertinent topic from the outline; in the upper right corner, the source number from the bibliography card; and following his notes, the page number or numbers where the information has been found.

Sample notecards:

Evidences in RBOC – Animalistic Behavior ③

"He [Henry] was not going to be badgered of his life like a kitten chased by boys."

p. 85

Naturalism – Major tenets ②

Man is "... at the mercy of superior social and cosmic forces and of his own instincts."

p. xi

---

a denial of freedom of the will.

p. 194 ①

It will be noted that notes from more than one source may be entered on a single card. If the note from one source is rather brief, as it is on the second sample, then notes from another source may be added. It is important, though, that a line be drawn to separate the two sources and that the second source number be placed in the right corner.

Accuracy in note-taking cannot be over-emphasized. The omission of one small detail, such as the source number or the page number, may mean wearisome hours spent in trying to obtain information which could readily have been gotten the first time. Although it is certainly permissible to write on both sides of the card, the student will find it advantageous not to do so. He will find that the handling of the cards, especially when it comes to the actual writing of the paper, will be facilitated by having notes on one side only. All notes should be taken in ink since pencil will smudge. The student should not type his notes; it is impractical and a waste of time. It is unlikely that the student will have his typewriter with him wherever he goes or, for that matter, that he will be able to use it in the library while using reserve books or periodicals. As for taking notes to be typed later, this is nothing more than wasteful duplication. It is far better to take notes neatly and legibly once.

TYPES OF NOTES: There are five basic types of notes that the student can take on his reading, and it is imperative that he be familiar with all of them. Since the reading of his sources is the essential element in the preparation of the paper, it is the calibre and accuracy of his notes which will, to a great measure, determine the quality of his final product. (See Appendix I for samples of the different types of notecards.)

The five types of notes are: *direct quotations, paraphrase, précis and summary, outline,* and *personal reactions to and comments on the readings.* Of course, these types are not mutually exclusive and may be used in combination. Let us now look at each one of these individually.

Direct quotation[1]: In his reading, the student will come across ideas which are so effectively expressed that changing the wording would affect the impact of the statement. In addition, he may be impelled to quote where the meaning may be changed if he were to paraphrase. It may be well to caution the student at this point against overquoting and using lengthy quotations which generally add little to the paper except monotony. A careful paraphrase that does complete justice to the source is preferable to a lengthy quotation.

As the student is doing his reading, he must determine if the information warrants being quoted. If he is in doubt, yet feels that the statement could possibly be quoted, he should copy the item verbatim, for he can always paraphrase it in his paper. Once he has decided to quote, he must exercise the greatest care to copy the original exactly, including any errors, and to place the entire statement in quotation marks. Since he will be quoting only part of a selection, he must also be positive that by taking the statement out of context he is not changing the basic meaning, tone, or intent of the author.

It is most important that he remember to indicate the page number or numbers from which he quoted since failure to acknowledge his source in his paper would be considered plagiarism. If the quotation in the original source continues onto a second page, a slash (/) may be used to indicate the page division, although it is not necessary.

Occasionally, the student will find that the source he is using is quoting some other source. Although it is always best to go back to the primary source, there will be times when the student must make use of this secondary source.

---

[1] For a detailed discussion of types of quotation and the mechanics of punctuation, see Chapter VII.

In so doing, he must be sure that he transcribes this quotation in single quotation marks and specifies, in addition to the page number, the original source.

There are three particular problems that the student might encounter when using quotations: (1) If there is some error in the quoted passage, *sic* (Latin for "thus") should be placed in brackets following the error to indicate that the error is in the original. However, the term should not be overused. Passages written in sub-standard English, or in fifteenth-century English should not be strewn with *sic's*. (2) If there is some information that the student wants to insert within the quoted matter, he must place it within brackets, and the insertion must conform grammatically and structurally to the quotation. *Parentheses may not be substituted for the brackets.* (3) If there is some part of the quotation that the student wants to omit, he may do so—as long as the omission does not affect the meaning or tone of the quotation—by indicating the ellipsis with three spaced dots (. . .).

Paraphrase: If the exact phrasing of the statement is not important, then the material should be paraphrased, that is, restated in the student's own words. A paraphrased statement will be approximately the same length as the original. To avoid the possibility of using the author's words with some minor changes, the student should carefully read the passage to be paraphrased, then close the text and write down the statement.

Here, too, page numbers must be indicated. Even though the statement has not been quoted, the source must be acknowledged.

Précis and summary: The bulk of the notes will be in either précis or summary form. The précis is a condensation of the original (usually one-fourth to one-third of the length), retaining, for the most part, the author's style, tone, point of view, and, very frequently, his words. What the student eliminates are the illustrations, the detailed explanations, and anything else he can which will permit him to express the gist of the passage. The summary, on the other hand, is the gist of a passage stated in the student's own words with no attempt made to retain the original tone, style, or point of view.

The student will find that since his research will not be limited to facts alone, but will incorporate ideas as well, he must be able to comprehend these ideas and incorporate them into his thinking. Taking copious notes is not the best way of accomplishing this. It can be more effectively done by concentrating on the selection, laying the source aside, thinking the ideas through, and *then* writing the précis or summary. After the notes have been written, he should check them against the source to make sure that the facts and ideas were not inadvertently misstated. Page numbers must be indicated just as for direct quotations and paraphrased statements.

Outline: In lieu of the summary, the outline, highlighting major ideas of a longer passage, may be used to good advantage. This form, however, should be used sparingly, and when used, should conform to correct ouline format.

Personal reactions and comments: Since the student will be relying solely on his notecards when writing the paper, he will find it to his advantage to jot down his personal comments and reactions to the information from his sources. This is highly recommended since it is best to write down one's reactions the moment they occur. No matter how strong the reaction is at the time, it might be difficult to recall months later. However, he must devise some method to distinguish his comments from the notes on the sources. Several possibilities exist, among these the use of a different color ink, printing one's observations where all other notes are written in script, or boxing one's comments. Any method is all right as long as it is readily distinguishable from the other notes and the student uses it consistently.

The reading of the sources and note-taking is the most time-consuming—and most rewarding—part of research. The student should again be cautioned to exercise great care with this phase of his research. If he is to avoid duplication of his efforts and if he is to avoid possible charges of inaccuracy or plagiarism, he must constantly be on the alert against carelessness and slovenliness. In addition, to insure proper focus on his topic, he must check his preliminary outline for possible revision.

Once he has completed taking his notes, his research, for all intents and purposes, has been completed; nothing remains but the writing of his results.

CHAPTER V

WRITING THE PAPER

The time has now come when the student must sit down and write the paper. If he has carefully followed all the procedures outlined thus far, this will not be as formidable a task as it might seem. While doing his reading, he kept revising his preliminary outline, adding topics, deleting others, condensing some and expanding others —at the same time making corresponding changes in the topics on his notecards—so that now his preliminary outline is, for the most part, the outline of his paper. Now, working from his notes and taking into consideration his audience, his point of view, his tone, and his purpose, he is ready to begin his first draft.

WORKING FROM THE NOTECARDS: Since he has been constantly revising his outline while keeping his statement of thesis in mind, the student's notes will reflect his outline. All that remains for him to do is to organize these cards into groups in accordance with the topic headings and then organize the cards within these groups in the order in which he wants to deal with them. It is here that the extra care and time devoted to taking neat notes on cards will pay off. It will not be necessary for him to devote long hours to several readings of his notes, to revising notes, to circling and tagging items as he would have had to do had he taken them helter-skelter on long sheets of paper. The notes are organized and neat, and all that remains is for him to "shuffle" them into the proper sequence. Then the student has only to spread a group of cards before him to see at a glance what information he has available. Of course, he must realize that there is no need for him to make use of *all* the notes he has taken. If he has done his job well, he will have more notes than are necessary. This is not only to be expected but is desirable.

THE FIRST DRAFT: Before beginning to write, the student should again clarify for himself what his primary objective is so that everything in the paper is directed towards that end. This objective must either be stated or implied in his introduction, the length of which is determined by the total length of the paper; the longer the paper, the longer the introduction. (A preface or formal introduction usually is not necessary in shorter papers —2000 to 3000 words—but is recommended in the longer ones, especially in theses.) It is here that the reader will be informed of the purpose, tone, and attitude of the writer so that he will be able to follow the argument in the body easily.

The body of the paper—the development of the introduction is—of course, the most important and longest part. It is here that the student presents, in an organized, coherent, unified, forceful manner, all the material which he has spent countless hours gathering. However, he must be cautious not to present a "scissors and paste" project; he must do more than simply report facts gleaned from his reading or a compilation of other people's thinking. The value of a paper is not judged by the number of footnotes present or by the number of quotations used. If the paper is to have merit and if it is to stimulate a reader, it must be written so that it reflects the student's careful consideration and understanding of his readings, his contemplation of what he has read, and his own thinking on the subjects, all leading to a sound conclusion.

The length of the conclusion will, like the introduction, be determined by the length of the body. It may range from a paragraph in the short paper to a full chapter in the thesis. Whatever the length, it should never be necessary for the writer to say "in conclusion." The ending should so logically sum up the material presented that there can be no doubt that this is the end.

Students who write their first draft in longhand should use widelined paper and a pen. They should write on alternate lines or on every third line, thus leaving ample room for revisions. They should also leave ample margins on both left and right, and number the pages consecutively. Students should write clearly and legibly, paying attention to proper sentence structure, paragraphing, spelling, and grammar, but not to the point where it will interfere with their concentration on the content. Once they have utilized some information from their notecards, they should check off these items.

Those students who find it easier to type their first drafts should double or triple space, leaving wide margins on all four sides. Since this will be a rough draft, they may find it easier to cross out errors than to erase. The ideal, of course, is to simplify the writing process by using a word processor. Anyone who has ever used one knows that correcting, inserting, deleting, and moving text requires little effort and eliminates the need for time-consuming rewriting. It will also simplify the writing and placing of footnotes.

Regardless of whether the student writes or types his first draft, he should first be sure that he has certain essential references at his side. Of paramount importance is a good dictionary (one which has recently been revised). In addition, he will find Roget's *Thesaurus* and a good writer's handbook on grammar and usage of great value in his writing. Whenever he is in doubt, he should not hesitate to utilize these sources. The student will find that if he pays attention to the mechanical and grammatical aspects of his first draft, he will be able to concentrate on the important element of style in his revision.

The first draft should be complete, though necessarily unpolished. It is important to make a draft of the title page, introductory pages, table of contents, and bibliography for these too may need revision before the final paper is completed.

COHERENCE AND UNITY: In order for a piece of writing to be readily understood by a reader, it must be unified and coherent. That is to say, every item, every thought must be relevant to the primary thesis and all these items must be logically related to each other.

The unity of a paper is maintained by carefully organizing one's thoughts into paragraphs—each paragraph expressing a separate idea through a series of related sentences developing the idea which was expressed or implied in the topic sentence. The student must be sure that each paragraph—and each sentence in the paragraph—is relevant to his major thesis. If he finds that any idea does not aid in the development of the thesis, then that idea—regardless of how interesting it may be in its own right—does not belong in a unified paper.

Unity in a paper does not necessarily imply coherence. Coherence can be achieved by several techniques: use of transitional words or phrases (such as *on the other hand, in addition, nevertheless, furthermore*); repetition of key thoughts, words, or phrases; partial restatement of ideas; use of synonyms for key words; use of parallel grammatical structure; consistent use of the same point of view; and logical organization of the information and arguments. It is the coherence which will enable the reader to follow the writer's argument easily and logically.

After the writer has asked himself whether each thought and idea is relevant to the thesis statement and whether it *adds* something to that which has already been said, he should ask one additional question: Does it logically follow that which precedes it and is it properly joined to the thought or idea that follows it? If the answer is yes, then his paper will be coherent.

POINT OF VIEW: Point of view is the term generally used to indicate the point from which the paper is written, that is, first person or third person. In very formal papers, the first person, singular, "I," is not generally used, the writer referring to himself in the third person, singular, e.g., "the author," "the researcher," "the writer." In less formal papers, the writer may sometimes make use of the first person, plural, the editorial "we." However, usage leans more and more toward the less formal and stiff "I." Unless the student's instructor or advisor has some definite objection, the first person "I" is highly recommended.

SOME ASPECTS OF STYLE: This section makes no attempt to present a complete discussion of all aspects of style nor does it pretend to be a grammar and usage text. For a reference source that will deal with all aspects of style, grammar, and correct usage, the student should refer, as frequently as necessary, to a good grammar text. In all probability, his freshman English handbook will serve the purpose. All that is intended here is to make the student cognizant of some of the more troublesome areas.

Sentence structure:

(a) *Errors in structure*: Two of the most common errors in sentence structure, the run-on or comma splice and the fragment, must be avoided at all costs. To be sure, either one of these can be used stylistically, but the writer must exercise the greatest caution. The run-on and fragment when used correctly are very effective, but if used incorrectly are very serious errors.

The run-on is primarily an error in punctuation; that is to say, two thoughts are run together without proper punctuation separating these thoughts. The run-on sentence can be corrected in three ways: (1) by placing a period at the end of the first thought and capitalizing the first word of the second thought; (2) by placing a semi-colon between the two thoughts; (3) by using a comma *and* a coordinating conjunction (*and, but, for, nor, or, yet, so*) between the two thoughts.

The fragment is an incompletely stated thought whose incompletion may be due to the omission of the subject, the verb, or the complement. It may also be due to using a verbal in place of a verb or by not completing a thought begun with a dependent clause. In any case, the fragment is corrected by supplying the missing part.

Other errors in structure include the dangling or misplaced modifier, awkward phrasing, and lack of parallelism. If the writer suspects that his sentence contains any one of these errors, he should refer to his handbook for proper methods of correction.

(b) *Subordination*: Subordination is the technique of placing the less important thought in a subordinate position. The dominant idea should always be expressed in the main clause. Subordinate clauses can be adverbial, adjectival, or substantive in function. In other words, these groups of words, containing a subject and verb, can function in the sentence in the same manner as an adverb, adjective, or noun. Subordinate thoughts which are not important enough to contain subject and verb should be expressed in phrases.

(c) *Variety*: It is variety in sentence structure and sentence opening which avoids monotony, makes the paper more readable, and enables the writer to express himself more effectively through the nuances in meaning reflected by the structure.

Basic structure of the sentence can be varied by compounding ideas or subordinating one idea to another. It can further be effected by using items in series; by using a series of short sentences; by effective use of involved, involuted sentence structure; by rearranging the normal subject-verb-complement pattern, and by varying sentence length.

Variations of sentence openings can be achieved by beginning a sentence with an adverbial clause, a prepositional phrase, a verbal (participle, gerund, infinitive) phrase, an expletive (a word such as *there* which has no grammatical function in the sentence), a parenthetical expression (*in fact, on the other hand*), an adverb, an adjective, or a coordinate conjunction. The student should be cautioned that although any of the above will give him variety, they cannot be used interchangeably, for each variation will affect the meaning of the sentence.

Abbreviations: Abbreviations should *not* be used in research papers, with the exception of the names of well-known organizations (after the name has been written out once) and for certain instances in footnote and bibliographic entries.

Numbers: Generally, all numbers which consist of one or two words are written out. In addition, *any* number which is the first word in a sentence must also be written out.

Numerals are to be used for (1) numbers consisting of more than two words, (2) numbers used in tabulations, (3) numbers used in statistical discussions, (4) sums of money, (5) numbers used in addresses and dates, (6) numbers used to express time of day when used with A.M. and P.M., but not with *o'clock*, and (7) page numbers, volume numbers, and chapter and verse numbers.

Italics: Italics in typed and hand-written manuscripts are indicated by underlining the item to be italicized with an unbroken line.

(a) *Emphasis*: Italics may be used (in lieu of quotation marks or capitalization) to stress a word or phrase in the text. However, they must be used sparingly if they are to be effective. When the writer wishes to stress a word or phrase within a direct quotation, he may also use italics. But he must then state in brackets (not parentheses) that he has supplied the italics.

(b) *Foreign terms*: Foreign terms which have not been anglicized must be italicized. Since there is disagreement, in some cases, as to which terms have been anglicized, the writer should use a recent edition of a good dictionary as his guide.

(c) *Titles*: Titles of full-length books, newspapers, magazines, periodicals, unpublished manuscripts are italicized. Titles of works which are part of a collection are placed within quotation marks.

(d) *Italicized words in sources*: Words or phrases which appear in italics in the quoted source must be underlined when quoted.

Contractions: Contracted forms should *not* be used. The only exception occurs when they appear in material that the writer wishes to quote. In such instances, he should *not* use *sic*.

Syllabification: Whenever possible, words should not be hyphenated, that is, split, between two lines. Where it becomes an absolute necessity, the writer must be certain that the break occurs only at the end of a syllable.

Punctuation: The writer should refer to his handbook of grammar for all the rules for the proper use of punctuation marks. Here, however, are some rules which need special emphasis:

(a) *Final punctuation*: Only one final punctuation mark is used. At no time will there be a double period, or a question mark followed by a period. The only exception would occur where the sentence ends with an abbreviation; then the period indicating the abbreviated form is followed by the question mark or the exclamation point, but never by another period.

(b) *Punctuation preceding final quotation mark*: The comma and period *always precede* the final quotation mark. All other punctuation marks precede the final quotation

mark when they are part of the quotation, and follow the
mark when they are not.

(c) *Parentheses and brackets in quotations*: Brackets
and parentheses are not to be confused. Brackets are only
to be used for the insertion of editorial comment within
a quotation. Anything appearing within parentheses is part
of the original quotation.

(d) *Ellipsis*: The omission of any part of a quotation
is indicated by three spaced dots (...). When the omission occurs at the end of a sentence, a fourth dot represent-
ing the period is added.

Tense: For a detailed discussion of the function, form, and
correct use of tense, mood, and voice, the student must
again avail himself of his handbook. However, the following points are worthy of stress:

(a) *Past tense*: Generally speaking, most papers are
written in the past tense. Occasionally, however, the writer
may want to make use of the historical present to give
greater emphasis to his content. This form should be used
sparingly.

(b) *Present tense*: Aside from its use in the historical
present, the present tense is also employed in critical comments (except biographical references where the subject
is deceased), and in stating universal truths. There is a
distinct difference, for instance, between saying *"Hamlet
was one of the greatest plays"* and *"Hamlet is one of the
greatest plays."*

(c) *Consistency*: Although changes in tense are permissible, the writer must be careful not to shift the tense
haphazardly in his paper. Unnecessary shifts in tense, aside
from affecting clarity and style, will ruin the unity.

Reference of pronouns: The writer must exercise great
care to make sure that when using a pronoun he has
either stated or clearly implied a definite antecedent.
Pronouns must agree with their antecedents in person,

gender, and number. When using such indefinite pronouns as *anyone* or *someone*, the third person, singular, masculine (functioning as common gender) must be used. Some people, however, object to using a masculine pronoun to refer to both a male and female and prefer using the cumbersome *he/she*. Unless the college style sheet requires such usage, it is better to change the antecedent to a plural noun and then use the appropriate third person plural pronoun.

Paragraphing: Since clarity of meaning is, to a great extent, dependent upon the logical expression of units of thought, the student must organize his paragraphs effectively. He should be aware of basic paragraph organization—topic sentence, development, concluding sentence—and of the various methods of paragraph development. He must also pay close attention to paragraph unity and coherence and to proper transition from one paragraph to the next.*

Vocabulary: Words convey meaning, and the broader the writer's vocabulary base, the easier he will be able to express his thoughts. The writer should be cautioned against a slavish dependence upon the *Thesaurus*, searching out "big" words because he feels that they will be impressive. Very often he will find that the word that best expresses his idea is the simplest one.

Spelling: When in doubt, the student should check his dictionary for the correct, preferred spelling, even if it means checking every word. The easiest way to check for spelling errors is with the word processor's spell-check program. This highlights all the misspelled words in the document, which should then be checked in a dictionary.

Wordiness: Student writers tend to be extremely verbose in the presentation of their ideas. Number of words alone does not reflect understanding, nor does it reflect thor-

---

*For a more detailed discussion of paragraph organization and development, see Chapter XII, pp. 106–113.

oughness in research or presentation of material. The student should be concise. If he finds that a paragraph can be condensed to one sentence or that the sentence can be condensed to a subordinate clause, the clause to a phrase, or the phrase to a word, or if the word can be eliminated altogether, the student should make the reduction. Then if he has a three-thousand-word paper, they will be three thousand meaningful words.

COPYREADING AND REVISION: After the first draft has been completed, it should be set aside for several days so that the writer can approach it with a degree of objectivity. If he re-reads the paper immediately, he will discover that he is not actually reading what he has written, but what he thinks he has written.

In copyreading his paper, the student should consciously check for all errors in grammar, mechanics, structure, and style. He should not hesitate to re-write whole portions of his paper if it is warranted. He should check for accuracy of his quotations, proper documentation, and inadvertent plagiarism. He should make sure that he has presented his material and his argument forcefully and coherently. He should check his facts against his notes. In short, the copyreading must take into account all aspects of content, structure, and style. Before he begins writing his final manuscript, there should not be slightest doubt in his mind that this is one of the best pieces of research and writing he has done.

CHAPTER VI

THE FORMAT OF THE RESEARCH PAPER

Once the student has completed his first draft and has made all necessary revisions and corrections—which might necessitate the re-writing of the paper in either part or whole—he is ready to write his final draft. (See Chapter XI.) It is at this point that the question of correct format arises. Although basic format varies very infrequently, the student should be certain to check with his instructor or advisor for any special instructions or variation in the form.

Generally speaking, research papers consist of three parts: (1) material(s) preceding the text, (2) the text, and (3) references and appendixes. The length of any of these three parts is determined by the length of the content and the extensiveness of the research. To be sure, in the short paper, materials preceding the text may consist of nothing more than the title page, and the references and appendixes will be limited to a listing of sources consulted in the preparation of the paper.

The following is the order in which the various items under each of the parts must be listed:

1. Materials preceding the text

    a.   Title-page (followed by a blank page)

    b.   Preface, including acknowledgments

    c.   Table of contents

    d.   List of tables

    e.   List of illustrations

2. Text

     a. Introduction
     b. Body of the paper
     c. Conclusion

3. References and appendixes

     a. References consulted in the preparation of the paper
     b. Other sources pertinent to the topic
     c. Appendixes

Although items under (1) and (3) may be omitted, the above sequence must be followed

MATERIALS PRECEDING THE TEXT: (For samples, see Appendix I.)

(a) Title page: The title page must contain the following information: (1) the title of the paper, (2) the name of the writer, (3) the name of the course for which the paper was written, (4) the name of the college, and (5) the date the paper is due. Of course, some colleges may require additional information.

In those instances where the college or instructor does not specify a particular title-page format, the above information should be attractively placed on the sheet. The best practice to follow is to place the title of the paper centered on the page in either upper case or upper-lower case letters. If the title is too long to be centered on one line, it should be written in inverted pyramid form without, however, splitting words or phrases. Titles should not be underlined or placed within quotation marks. Below the title, the writer should place his full name—first name then last name. In the lower left-hand corner he should indicate the course for which the paper is being written, and to the right of this, next to the right-hand margin, the name of the college and, below it, the due date.

(b) Preface: The preface, sometimes referred to as the foreword, is a brief statement of the scope, aim, and general character of the research. It should not be confused with the introduction which is an essential part of the text. The preface follows the blank sheet after the title-page and is headed PREFACE. In most short papers a preface is superfluous. If the student is not writing a preface but wishes to make acknowledgments, he should head a sheet ACKNOWLEDGMENTS rather than PREFACE.

(c) Table of contents: The table of contents is necessary only in those papers where the text has been divided into chapters. Here again, shorter papers will, in all probability, not require a table of contents.

Where a table of contents is necessary, the heading TABLE OF CONTENTS should be centered on the sheet and typed in upper case letters. Under the heading *Chapter,* at the left margin, chapter numbers are listed in large Roman numerals, aligned by the period following each numeral. Chapter headings are capitalized throughout. Page numbers are listed at the right margin in Arabic numerals under the heading *Page.*

Although sub-titles do not have to be included in the table of contents, it is highly recommended that the writer do so. Sub-titles enable the reader to see the basic outline of the work at a glance, and just as the researcher no doubt found this a boon in the preparation of the paper, so will his reader. When the sub-titles are listed, they are typed in upper-lower case letters (the first letter of the first word and all nouns, pronouns, adjectives, adverbs, and verbs are capitalized). All headings and sub-titles must correspond exactly with the headings as they appear in the body of the paper.

(d) List of tables: Where several tables have been included in the text, the writer must prepare a list of tables which follows the table of contents. The heading, LIST OF TA-

BLES, should be centered on the sheet and typed in capitals. Under the heading *Table*, at the left, table numbers are listed in Arabic numerals; the corresponding page numbers are listed under *Page* at the right-hand margin. Next to the table number, the title of the table is typed in upper-lower case letters. No list of tables is necessary where only one or two tables have been included in the text.

(e) List of illustrations: The list of illustrations will be in the same form as the list of tables. The sheet will be headed LIST OF ILLUSTRATIONS, and the numbers of the illustrations, in Arabic numerals, will be listed at the left margin; the illustration title will be in upper-lower case letters; and the page numbers will be in Arabic numerals at the right-hand margin. Here again, one or two illustrations in the text will not necessitate the inclusion of a list of illustrations.

THE TEXT: The text is, of course, the most important part of the paper, for it is here that the writer presents his facts and his argument. The more logically, coherently, and effectively he can do this, the better his chance of enlightening his reader and, where it is part of his overall purpose, of convincing him. It becomes, therefore, imperative that the writer devote the major portions of his energy to a careful organization and presentation of his findings.

(a) Introduction: Whether the introduction is one paragraph or a separate chapter, it is the reader's first actual contact with the thoughts and writing style of the writer. If we are to assume that the reader is under no compulsion to read the paper, then the only criterion which will cause him to continue reading is sustained interest. If the introduction is dull, redundant, or confusing, the reader, if he has any sense at all, will simply put the text down. We must remember that there is absolutely nothing which will force a reader back to a paper once he has rejected it. The opening, therefore, must be vivid, interesting and stimulating; it must capture the reader's attention.

The length of the introduction will be determined by the overall length of the paper. The shorter papers (2000-3000 words) need little more than a well-developed introductory paragraph; the longer papers may need chapter-length introductions.

Where the introduction is chapter-length, the page is headed CHAPTER I with the chapter title, INTRODUCTION or some other descriptive title, below it. In those instances where the introduction is short but where the paper has been divided into chapters, the writer may prefer to simply head it INTRODUCTION without a chapter designation. In either case, however, the introduction is part of the text.

(b) Body of the paper: The main part of the text focuses on the development of the aims stated or implied in the introduction. Careful organization, adequate substantiation, and proper documentation will aid in developing a logical and forceful argument. In longer papers where chapter divisions are a necessity, each main idea will begin on a new page headed with the chapter number and the title of the chapter in upper-case letters. In the shorter papers, where there is no formal introduction, the argument should be developed without chapter divisions.

(c) Conclusion: Just as the introduction is of prime importance in making the reader aware of what he will read about, so the conclusion is important in tying together all that he has read. Since the conclusion is the last part to be read, it, too, must be forceful, giving the reader the distinct impression of having gained something positive from his reading. The conclusion, as the introduction, may be either part of the paper or a separate chapter. In those instances where the conclusion is a separate chapter, it must be assigned a chapter number and a title, which may be CONCLUSION. A more descriptive title is preferred, however.

REFERENCES AND APPENDIXES—(a) References consulted: Following the text, the student should list the sources he has consulted in the preparation of the paper. This bibliography should not contain all the sources that were examined but only those that had some definite bearing on the subject. If the bibliography is comparatively short, all entries are arranged alphabetically, by author's last name, under the page heading BIBLIOGRAPHY or SOURCES CONSULTED. In longer bibliographies, sources are generally separated into two categories: texts and periodicals. If this practice is followed, then the sub-headings *1. Texts* and *2. Periodicals* precede *each* grouping. The page heading remains as indicated above.

(b) Other sources: On occasion a writer may wish to supply a listing of works which the reader may consult for a more detailed and expanded study of the general topic. In such cases, he will list these works under the heading of SUPPLEMENTARY BIBLIOGRAPHY or ADDITIONAL SOURCES. These works will be listed in alphabetical order by author's last name. (For a more detailed discussion of bibliographies, and for sample entries, see Chapter IX.)

(c) Appendixes: The appendix serves the very useful function of permitting the writer to present additional information which is interesting and related to the topic but yet not pertinent enough to be incorporated within the text. Here may be included such things as additional tables, sample questionnaires used in the study, copies of documents used but not generally available, and additional illustrative materials. If these items are comparatively short, they may be listed under a single APPENDIX heading. If, on the other hand, each of these categories is extensive, then the writer should number his appendixes and present each kind of material in a separate appendix. It is up to the writer to decide whether he will place the appedixes before or after the bibliography.

PAGINATION: Every page in a research paper except the blank sheet following the title page is assigned a number.

From the title page up to, but not including, the first page of the research paper, small Roman numerals are used *at the bottom* of the page to designate the page number. These numerals are centered on the line and enclosed by dashes (e.g., -iv-). Although the title page is actually page -i-, it is *not* numbered. Therefore, the first page of the materials preceding the text will be numbered -ii-.

All other pages of the research paper, starting with the first page of the text, are numbered with Arabic numerals centered *at the top* of the page and enclosed by dashes. An exception in the placement of page numbers occurs for pages with chapter headings, including such headings as bibliography and appendix. Here the page number is centered on the line *at the bottom* of the page.

TITLES AND SUB-TITLES: Where the paper is divided into chapters, the writer may head each new chapter CHAPTER, followed with the appropriate number in large Roman numerals. This is centered on the line and below that is placed the chapter title in upper-case letters. The student may prefer to eliminate the word *chapter* and place the Roman numeral immediately preceding the title.

Regardless of which method is used, each chapter must begin on a separate page with a concise, vivid chapter heading. Chapter headings must either clearly state or imply the contents of that which follows. Should the title be long, it must be divided and centered in an inverted pyramid. End punctuation other than the question and exclamation marks is not used.

The placement of sub-titles will depend on the number of sub-divisions in any given chapter. If the writer is using only one rank of sub-division, the sub-title is then placed at the margin, followed by a period and a dash, and is italicized. If there is to be a further sub-division, then the first sub-title is centered on the line and italicized, and the second sub-title is placed at the margin. All sub-titles centered on the line are written in upper-lower case; titles placed at the margin are written in lower case except for the first letter of the first word, which is capitalized. All titles should be concise, pertinent, and descriptive.

Perhaps it is best again to make the student aware that there are possible variations in pagination, chapter headings, and sub-titles, and that in the final analysis he must be guided by the wishes of his instructor or by the college style sheet. Where no specific instructions are given, he should follow the procedure outlined herein.

CHAPTER VII

QUOTATIONS

In taking his notes, the student may frequently have decided to copy certain information *verbatim* from his sources. Now, while writing his paper, he must determine which and how much of these quotations he will incorporate. The novice writer may well succumb at this point to quoting too freely, feeling that he can never express the ideas as effectively as the writer of the source. This, however, would be folly, for nothing contributes as much to dull writing as a series of long quotations connected by brief bridging passages. Furthermore, lengthy quotations may cause the reader to forget whether he is reading an excerpt or the writer's own ideas. It is best, then, to keep direct quotations as short as possible and to use them sparingly.

WHEN TO QUOTE: Although the actual decision of when to quote must be made by the student, taking into account the proposed quotation and the context in which it will be used, there are certain guidelines he can follow. If he finds that any changes in the phrasing would alter the author's meaning or effect, he should quote the passage. However, this decision is not simply based on the student's inability to state the idea as well stylistically; the paraphrase would have to be detrimental to the overall effect of the passage in order to warrant the student's quoting it directly. The passage should also be quoted where the changes in phrasing of the author's description of a procedure might cause misunderstanding.

In both instances as well as in any other instance where the student may decide to quote, he must be guided by the principle that a careful paraphrase that does complete justice to the source is preferable to a lengthy quotation. Furthermore, he should avoid quotations which run to several paragraphs. In many instances, there is not even a need to quote complete sentences. The writer can just as readily quote the pertinent part of the statement and incorporate it within his own sentence structure. To be sure, direct quotations do tend to enhance the paper and to lend it greater validity, but only when they are used with discretion.

DIRECT PROSE QUOTATIONS: Short direct prose quotations—usually no longer than two sentences—should be included in the text enclosed in double quotation marks. When a quotation occurs within the passage being quoted, that portion is to be placed within single quotation marks.

Original: The old man, shoving up the front of his tarpaulin and deliberately rubbing the long slant scar at the point where it entered the thin hair, laconically said, "Baby Budd, *Jemmy Legs*" (meaning the master-at-arms) "is down on you."

Quoted: "The old man, shoving up the front of the tarpaulin and deliberately rubbing the long slant scar at the point where it entered the thin hair, laconically said, 'Baby Budd, *Jemmy Legs*' (meaning the master-at-arms) 'is down on you.' "

Note that in the above example both single and double quotation marks are used, since there is dialogue within the quoted passage. However, if only the dialogue within the passage were quoted, only single quotation marks should be used:

Original: "And that's because he's down upon you, Baby Budd."

Quoted: 'And that's because he's down upon you, Baby Budd.'

When quotations are longer—two or more sentences and/or four or more typewritten lines—they should be set off from the text and indented both left and right. In double spaced manuscript, these longer quotations are single spaced and are *not* enclosed with quotation marks. It should be noted that the definition of "longer quotation" is somewhat arbitrary and may be modified. For emphasis, shorter quotations may also be set off from the text, but they should run to at least two typewritten lines. If the writer is using a word processor, he should set the quotation in smaller type.

Original: Villains, whatever fate befell them in the obligatory last panel, were infinitely better equipped than those silly, hapless heroes. Not only comics, but life taught us that. Those of us raised in ghetto neighborhoods were being asked to believe that crime didn't pay? Tell that to the butcher! Nice guys finished last; landlords, first. Villains by their simple appointment to the role were miles ahead. It was not to be believed that any ordinary human could combat them. More was required. Someone with a call. When *Superman* at last appeared, he brought with him the deep satisfaction of all underground truths: our reaction was less, "How original!" than, "But, of course!"

> *Quoted:* Villains, whatever fate befell them in the obligatory last panel, were infinitely better equipped than those silly, hapless heroes. Not only comics, but life taught us that. Those of us raised in ghetto neighborhoods were being asked to believe that crime didn't pay? Tell that to the butcher! Nice guys finished last; landlords first. Villains by their simple appointment to the role were miles ahead. It was not to be believed that any ordinary human could combat them. More was required. Someone with a call. When *Superman* at last appeared, he brought with him the deep satisfaction of all underground truths: our reaction was less, "How original!" than, "But, of course!"

Note that the quotation is an exact reproduction of the original. When a quotation appears within the passage, that quotation is placed within double quotation marks. Otherwise, *no* quotation marks are placed outside of the quoted passage.

Meticulous care must be taken to reproduce a quotation exactly. This means that it must be copied without any changes whatsoever. Every punctuation mark, every capitalization, every italicized word—even every spelling error—must be faithfully reproduced. However, to protect himself, the writer must indicate that the error in the passage—whether it be a misspelling or an obviously ungrammatical sentence—is not his own by placing the Latin word *sic* (meaning *thus*) in brackets immediately following the error. The term *sic* must be italicized. However, the term should not be overused. Passages written in substandard English or in Spenserian English, for example, should not be strewn with *sic*'s.

> *Original*: Television has become an important medium of communication in our modren society, and teachers would do well to recognize the valuable and important part this medium can play in the teaching program.
>
> *Quoted*: "Television has become an important medium of communication in our modren [*sic*] society, and teachers would do well to recognize the valuable and important part this medium can play in the teaching program."

When a passage runs to two or more paragraphs, each paragraph is preceded with double quotation marks, but closing quotation marks are placed only at the end of the last paragraph. This is true only when the quotation is double spaced. Setting off the passage from the text and single spacing is preferred.

POETRY QUOTATIONS: Quotations of verse that run to two or more lines should be set off from the text, single spaced, and centered on the line. No quotation marks are to be used unless they appeared in the original. Here again the writer must exercise meticulous care to reproduce the material exactly.

When short poetic quotations are included within the text, they are enclosed in double quotation marks. In this case, however, the end of the poetic line is indicated by the use of the slash, e.g., "Stone walls do not a prison make,/ Nor iron bars a cage." No slash is placed after the last line quoted. In setting off longer quotations from the text, the writer must also make certain that he follows the poet's indentations or visual arrangement of the lines. For example:

> If to be absent were to be
> > Away from thee;
> > Or that when I am gone,
> > You or I were alone,
> Then, my Lucasta, might I crave
> Pity from blustering wind or swallowing wave.

ELLIPSES: Omissions in quotations are permitted when the writer feels that the portion is not necessary. However, great care must be exercised that the tone, meaning, or intent of the passage is not altered. The symbol for the ellipsis is three spaced periods (...). When the ellipsis occurs at the end of the passage, a fourth period—the end punctuation mark— is added. When quotation marks are used, the ellipsis is always enclosed within the quotation marks.

> *Original*: Humble and rustic life was generally chosen, because, in that condition, the essential passions of the heart find a better soil in which they can attain their maturity, are less under restraint, and speak a plainer and more emphatic language.

> *Quoted*: "Humble and rustic life was generally chosen, because, in that condition, the essential passions of the heart ... speak a plainer and more emphatic language."

The ellipsis, of course, can occur at the beginning or at the end of the passage as well. Also there may be more than one ellipsis in any given passage. When the writer, in quoting two or more paragraphs or two or more stanzas, wishes to omit a complete paragraph or stanza, he indicates this omission by a single line of spaced periods.

The student, however, must again be cautioned about the careless use of ellipses. The omission of a single word can affect the meaning of an entire passage. Good scholarship and honesty demand that the writer check and re-check any passage in which an omission occurs to make certain that the meaning, tone, or intent has not been altered.

INTERPOLATION: There will be times when the writer will find it necessary to insert an explanation or correction into the quotation. All such editorial comments must be placed within brackets, *not parentheses.* Although it is preferred that brackets be typed in typewritten manuscripts, they may be inked in.

The most common interpolations are the supplying of antecedents and the use of *sic* to indicate some error in the quotation. On occasion, however, the writer may want to stress a word or phrase in the quoted passage by italicizing it. He must then indicate that the italics are his by stating "italics mine" or "emphasis added" within brackets following the emphasized word or phrase.

> *Supplying an antecedent*: "He [Henry Fleming] was not going to be badgered ... like a kitten chased by boys ...."

> *Correction noted*: "William Shakesper [*sic*] probably wrote *Macbeth* in 1606 as a tribute to James II [I]."

> *Emphasis within quotation*: "Crafty men condemn studies, simple men admire them, and wise men use them; for *they teach not their own use* [italics mine]; but that there is a wisdom without them, and above them, won by observation."

QUOTATION WITHIN WRITER'S SENTENCE: More often than not, the student will wish to quote only part of a passage and incorporate that within his own sentence structure. At such times, he must be certain that the quoted passage conforms to his own sentence structure and that pronoun reference and tense are consistent.

Original: And there were iron laws of tradition and law on four sides. He was in a moving box.

Quoted: Fleming instinctively looked for a way out but he was enclosed by the "... iron laws of tradition and law on four sides."

PUNCTUATING QUOTATIONS: The punctuation of quotations is in accord with two basic rules:

(1) Periods and commas *always precede* the end quotation mark, even when the item consists of a single word or letter, e.g., "animal," 1st." *There is no exception to this rule.*

(2) All other punctuation marks precede the end quotation mark when they are part of the quoted passage; when they are not, they follow the end quotation mark.

Examples:

"But why," he asked, "are you following this dangerous course?"

Does that mean we are condemning to death "... a fellow creature innocent before God..."?

Note that in the first example the quoted passage itself was an interrogative statement, but in the second example the quotation was not a question; rather it was the whole statement which was interrogative. In the case where both the quotation and the statement are questions, the question mark precedes the end quotation mark.

Another problem in punctuation is the mark preceding quotations. When the quotation is part of the writer's sentence structure, the punctuation marks used are those which are demanded by the basic structure of the sentence.

When, however, the quotation is introduced by an explanatory or narrative tag—such as "Wordsworth in the *Preface* stated"—the tag is followed by a comma. When the quotation introduced is lengthy—which means that it would be single spaced and set off from the text—it is preceded by a colon.

FOOTNOTING QUOTATIONS: All direct quotations must be documented. The only possible exception is in the case of familiar quotations. However, the student would be wise to document even these. The footnote numeral should follow the final punctuation mark, or quotation mark, of the direct quotation when the MLA format is not being used. (For footnoting procedures, see Chapter VIII.)

SECONDARY SOURCE QUOTATIONS: Ideally, the writer should not be making any use at all of secondary sources. However, this is not always practical. In those instances where the primary source is not available or easily accessible, the writer will have to rely on the secondary source. It is imperative, though, that in his footnote he not only list the source he consulted but also the primary source. When the primary source is quoted within the quoted secondary text, the material from the primary source must be placed within single quotation marks.

ETHICS OF QUOTING. The writer must keep uppermost in his mind that using someone else's words or ideas without giving proper credit is literary theft for which he is legally as well as morally liable. Whether the lack of credit or improper documentation is due to carelessness or to basic dishonesty is immaterial. Hence, the writer must exercise the greatest caution that when quoting he is doing so accurately, retaining the author's words, punctuation (the omission of a comma might change the meaning), and tone. This is especially true when he makes use of ellipses. In other words, the writer must check, re-check, and double check every quotation he uses against the source. Then, and only then, can he be reasonably certain of having done justice to the author.

CHAPTER VIII

DOCUMENTING SOURCES

Documenting sources is an important adjunct to the research paper. Here the writer can credit his sources and lend greater credence to his argument by indicating them. Although the writer has some latitude in determining what to document, there are certain guidelines. However, the value of a paper is not judged by the number of sources documented, so he should use these with discretion.

The two basic methods currently being used for documenting sources are the MLA and University of Chicago formats. The MLA style incorporates references to the sources parenthetically within the text. Since footnotes are not used, the reader is not interrupted. Although MLA style is generally preferred, students should also be familiar with the University of Chicago format since often sources in one's own research use this style.

When using the University of Chicago format, the student is urged to write his footnotes during the preparation of his first draft. In this way he will be able to ascertain the need for additional data that might have to be incorporated in the note. Also it will allow him to proofread the notes and discover any errors in content or form so that he can make any necessary corrections.

PURPOSE OF DOCUMENTING SOURCES: Footnotes may be classified according to two types: reference and content. Reference notes give the publication facts of sources cited or make references to other parts of the paper. Content footnotes allow the writer to give additional information which he feels is of interest to the reader yet is not vital enough to be incorporated within the text.

Reference notes: Facts used in a research paper that are commonly known are public property and may be used without any acknowledgment; but any other fact or any idea that is not public property must be credited to the original author. The following items *must* be documented:

(1) Direct quotations.

(2) Statements which are paraphrased.

(3) All statements which are not generally accepted as true.

(4) Any opinion or idea which did not originate with the writer.

Prior knowledge on the part of the writer does not affect footnoting. That is to say even if he never knew a certain fact, and has just learned it, he would not need to footnote it if it is common knowledge.

In addition to the above-mandated footnotes, reference notes also include the "see-also" note. Here the writer may wish to call the reader's attention to additional information either in some other text or in some other part of his paper.

Content notes: Content footnotes are very akin to appendixes. Here the writer has the opportunity to expand, amplify, or comment on the information presented in the text. Here he may present interesting sidelights on the topic under discussion, quote additional sources, or expand the discussion with additional details. Regardless of what he incorporates here, he is restricted by the fact that the content note must be relevant, albeit tangential, to the topic under discussion in the text.

In writing the content note, the writer must be guided by good English. He must adhere to proper sentence structure, paragraphing, and coherence. If he makes reference to another source, he must give pertinent publication facts.

THE MLA STYLE: Before using this style for documenting his sources, the writer must have a complete bibliography so that its information matches the parenthetical references. (See Chapter 9 for bibliographic entries.) He then need give only enough information for the reader to readily locate the source. This information would include the author's name, if not mentioned already in the passage, and the page number(s) of the source.

Author's name in bibliography but not in passage: If there is only *one work by the author cited*, the writer need list only the author's last name (and the first initial if there is more than one author with the same last name). If there are *two or more works by the same author*, he must add the title, or a shortened version, after the author's name. If there are *two or three authors*, he must list the last name of each. If there are *more than three authors*, he must list the last name of the first author followed either by *et al.* or "and others." When there is *no author* listed, he must give the title or a shortened version thereof. Here are some examples:

One author: The "Bright Star" sonnet was originally written to Mrs. Isabella Jones (Daiches 338).

Two or more works by the same author: "Now, with the newborn question in his mind, he was compelled to sink back into his old place as part of a blue demonstration" (Crane, *Red Badge* 12).

Two or three authors: Ellen Terry gave the crushing reply to all literary detective work when she argued that, by the same criteria, Shakespeare must have been a woman (Wellek and Warren 67).

No author listed: At night he went to see how the Danes had acted after the beer banquet ("Beowulf" 5).

When the passage being documented contains more than one sentence, the source citation *follows* the end punctuation mark. If, however, the passage being documented is part of a sentence, then the citation follows that part.

Author's name in passage: When the author's name has been mentioned in the passage, the writer need give only the page number(s):

Ellen Terry, according to Wellek and Warren, gave the crushing reply to all literary detective work when she argued that, by the same criteria, Shakespeare must have been a woman (67).

Documenting quotations: For short quotations the source information *follows* the end quotation mark but *precedes* the period. For longer quotations, two or more sentences and/or four or more typed lines set off from the text, the source information follows the end punctuation of the quoted passage.

Secondary source citations: If the primary source is not available, it may be necessary to use the secondary source. In that case, *qtd. in* (quoted in), if it is a direct quotation, or *ctd. in* (cited in), if it is not, precedes the secondary source citation. (It is advisable to document the primary source in a content footnote.) For example:

As John F. Kennedy so eloquently stated in his Inaugural Address, '. . . ask not what America can do for you, but what together we can do for the freedom of man' (qtd. in Quinn and Dolan 62).

The writer should give sufficient information to enable the reader to locate a passage easily. This may necessitate incorporating chapter, stanza, lines, and even primary source data within the parentheses.[1]

---

[1]For a more detailed discussion of the MLA style, see Joseph Gibaldi and Walter S. Achtert, *MLA Handbook for Writers of Research Papers* (New York: The Modern Language Association of America, 1988).

UNIVERSITY OF CHICAGO STYLE: Although the MLA style is relatively new and much simpler to use, it is important for the student to familiarize himself with the University of Chicago format since it has been in use for a long time, and especially if one's instructor or university mandates it. Students will also find it helpful in their research to understand such entries as *ibid.*, *op. cit.*, *loc. cit.*, and *passim*.

PLACING AND NUMBERING OF FOOTNOTES: Footnotes may be placed in any one of three places: at the bottom of the page, at the end of the chapter, or at the end of the paper, in which case they are called *endnotes*. Placement at the bottom of the page is preferred. The footnotes are there for the convenience of the reader. Everyone has been annoyed by having to turn to the end of the text for a footnote only to discover that it was a source citation. When footnotes appear at the bottom of the page, the reader need only glance down to see whether the note is of interest to him.

All footnote references—with the exception of those in mathematical texts where a footnote number may be mistaken for an exponent—use Arabic numerals. Although notes may be renumbered on each page, they generally are numbered consecutively throughout each chapter. Where the paper is not divided into chapters, footnotes should be numbered consecutively throughout. The footnote number is placed *following* the statement—and the punctuation mark—to which the note refers. It is raised one-half space and is *not* followed by a period or enclosed in dashes or parentheses, nor is it circled.

Every footnote number in the text must be represented by a correspondingly numbered note at the bottom of the page. These footnotes are separated from the text by a double space and a solid line from the left-hand margin and as long as the longest line on that page. Footnote entries are single spaced with a double space between them.

Where footnote numbers might be confused with mathematical figures, the writer must use a series of symbols, e.g., the asterisk, cross, or double cross, which must be re-used on every page where information is to be documented.

FIRST MENTION OF A REFERENCE: The first time a work is cited, it must include all the information necessary for easy location of the work. The footnote should include the author's full name, the title of the work, the facts of the publication, and the volume and page numbers. This information should be arranged as follows:

1. Author's first name, middle initial, and last name, followed by a comma.
2. Title of the book, underlined.
3. Place and date of publication, separated by a comma and enclosed in parentheses, followed by a comma.
4. Volume number, in large Roman numerals, followed by a comma.
5. Page number, followed by a period.

This data is then placed at the bottom of the page, immediately below the solid horizontal line. The footnote numeral is indented and raised, and the footnote is single spaced. Second and successive lines of the entry are brought to the left margin.

PUNCTUATION OF FOOTNOTES: The title of any work published separately must be underlined. Titles of works incorporated within a text are enclosed in quotation marks. Names of the books of the Bible, titles of ancient manuscripts, and legislative acts and bills are never underlined or placed within quotation marks.

All words in a title with the exception of prepositions, articles, and conjunctions are capitalized. The only exception occurs in cases like e e cummings' poetry, where the poet wrote the title in all lowercase letters. However, the student may capitalize such titles. A period is placed at the end of all footnote entries.

When a book title includes the title of a selection in the book, the selection title is placed within quotation marks and the entire title is underlined. (Note that anything underlined in a typed or handwritten manuscript will be set in italic when printed.) Conversely, when the title of an article, for example, includes the title of a book, the entire title is placed within quotation marks and the title of the book is underlined, e.g., "The Motif of the Wise Old Man in *Billy Budd.*"

PUBLICATION FACTS: The essential publication facts that should be included in the footnote entry are the place and date of publication. Inclusion of the publishing company is rather superfluous, since this fact can be found in the bibliography. Where more than one place of publication is listed in the source book, the first one—or the place geographically nearest—is to be used. The date of publication is the date of the first printing. In the case of a revised edition, the date of that edition should be listed.

The publication facts should have been indicated on the student's bibliography cards. If the information was inadvertently omitted, he will then have to get the source and check the title and copyright pages for this information.

EXAMPLES OF FOOTNOTE ENTRIES FOR FIRST REFERENCE TO A SOURCE:

Book—one author:

[1]Chaim Potok, *My Name Is Asher Lev* (New York, 1972), pp. 6–7.

Book—one author; numbered or revised edition:

[2]Kimball Wiles, *Supervision for Better Schools*, 3rd ed. (Englewood Cliffs, N. J., 1967), p. 156.

[*Note*: Since the place of publication given here is not generally known, the state must be indicated as well.]

Book—one author; more than one volume:

[3]Vernon Louis Parrington, *Main Currents in American Thought* (New York, c. 1930), vol. II, pp. 112-113.

[*Note*: Since this reference contains both a volume and a page number, it is permissible to omit "vol." and "pp." This information would be designated as "II, 112-113." The writer should determine the method he prefers and then use it consistently throughout his paper. Also note the notation "c. 1930." The "c." designates *copyright*, and the entry is an indication that no publication date was available. If no date could have been found, then "n.d." (no date) would follow the place of publication.]

Book—two authors:

[4]William H. Masters and Virginia E. Johnson, *Human Sexual Inadequacy* (Boston, 1970), p. iii.

[*Note*: Where two or more authors are given, authors' names are *not* arranged alphabetically but in the order in which they appear on the title page. Also note that the page number refers to materials preceding the text.]

Book—more than three authors:

[5]David Austin *et al.*, *Reading Rights for Boys*: *Sex Role and Development in Language Experience* (New York, 1971), p. 142.

[*Note*: In lieu of "*et al.*" the anglicized form "and others" may be used. Here again the student should determine which form he prefers and use that form consistently throughout his paper.]

Book—no author given:

[6]*The Lottery* (London, [1732]),pp. 9-10.

[*Note*: The brackets enclosing the publication date indicate that the date had been omitted from the title page and was located in the card catalog or some other reference work.]

Book—editor of a collection:

[7]John Hollander, ed., *Poems of Our Moment* (New York, 1968), p. 19.

[*Note*: The abbreviation "ed." or "eds." may be placed within parentheses. If this is done, the comma following the editor's name is omitted. The above entry should be used only when reference is made to the book as a whole and not to any selections within the book. See sample footnotes 11 and 12.]

Book—author and editor:

[8]Stephen Crane, *The Red Badge of Courage*, ed. Richard Chase (Boston, c. 1960), pp. 21-22.

Book—translated into English:

[9]Gustave Flaubert, *Madame Bovary,* trans. Gerard Hopkins (New York, 1959), pp. 215-216.

Book—no author or editor; translated:

[10]*The Anglo-Saxon Chronicle*, trans. G. N. Garmonsway (London, 1953), p. 131.

Book—article or essay by one of several contributors:

[11]Paul Goodman, "Growing Up Absurd — 'Human Nature' and the Organized System," *The Sense of the 60's*, eds. Edward Quinn and Paul J. Dolan (New York, 1968), pp. 9-10.

Book—selection in a collection by one author:

[12]Eldridge Cleaver, "The Allegory of the Black Eunuchs," *Soul on Ice* (New York, 1968), p. 159.

[*Note*: If there were an editor of the text, his name would follow the title, as in sample footnote 11, above.]

Article or essay—author given:

[13]Terry Southern, "The Rolling Stones' U.S. Tour: Riding the Lapping Tongue," *Saturday Review*, 55:25, August 12, 1972.

[*Note*: In the entry "55:25," the number preceding the colon is the volume number, and the number following the colon is the page number. An alternate form is given below.]

Article or essay—no author given:

[14]"South Viet Nam: Campaign of Brutality," *Time*, 100:17-18, August 21, 1972.

Article or essay—no author given; name supplied:

[15][Virginia Adams], "Teen-Age Sex: Letting the Pendulum Swing," *Time*, 100:35, August 21, 1972.

Article or essay—initials of author given; full name supplied:

[16]S[ebastian] H. G[unner], "Heresy in Education," *Journal of Educational Discourse*, 15:26-27, September, 1958.

Article or essay—alternate entry:

[17]Terry Southern, "The Rolling Stones' U.S. Tour: Riding the Lapping Tongue," *Saturday Review*, LV (August 12, 1972), 25.

Articles—encyclopedias, dictionaries, etc.:

[18]"Drama — Stories on the Stage," *Compton's Pictured Encyclopedia* (1967), IV, 169.

[*Note*: If the above were a numbered or revised edition, the edition number would precede the year, i.e., (4th ed., 1967).]

Newspaper:

[19]*New York Times*, September 7, 1972, Sec. 4, p. 3.

Newspaper—title and author given:

[20]Frank Taggart, "Clark Helps Revive Viet Issue," *Newsday* (Long Island), August 15, 1972, p. 5.

[*Note*: When the title of the newspaper does not include the place of publication, it should be included within parentheses following the title.]

Newspaper—title given; no author:

[21]"Republicans Start in Slugging," *Newsday* (Long Island), August 15, 1972, p. 3.

[*Note*: Whenever possible, the author and title of the article are given.]

Unpublished materials:

[22]Harry Teitelbaum, "A Study of Leisure-time Reading Habits of Second Year High School Students" (Unpublished Brooklyn College Master's Thesis, 1953), pp. 30-32.

Biblical reference:

[23]Matt. 2:5-8.

[*Note*: The number preceding the colon refers to the chapter; the numbers following, the verses.]

Bulletin—institution or organization as author:

[24]State University of New York at Stony Brook, *1971-72 Graduate Bulletin* (Stony Brook, 1971), pp. 49-50.

Lecture:

[25]John Sebastian, Lecture: "Naturalism in *The Red Badge of Courage*," Community Literary Discussion Group, September 23, 1964.

Secondary source quotation:

[26]Eldridge Cleaver, "The White Race and Its Heroes," *Soul on Ice* (New York, 1968), p. 65, quoting James Baldwin, *The Fire Next Time* (New York, 1963).

[*Note*: Whenever possible, complete publication facts of the primary source should be given. This information will generally be available in the author's footnote. Of course, it must be remembered that if the primary source is available to the student, he should refer to that rather than to the secondary source.]

Secondary source citation:

[27]John Jones, *Famous Authors and Their Works* (New York, 1945), p. 25, citing Nathaniel Hawthorne, *The Scarlet Letter* (Boston, 1850), pp. 4-5.

Secondary source citation or quotation—alternate:

[28]Nathaniel Hawthorne, *The Scarlet Letter* (Boston, 1850), pp. 4-5, cited by John Jones, *Famous Authors and Their Works* (New York, 1945), p. 25.

[*Note*: Either of these two forms is acceptable, but the writer should strive to be consistent in the form used within the paper.]

SECOND OR LATER MENTION OF A REFERENCE: After the first complete mention of a reference, later references to the source are made in shortened forms. This is true only when footnotes are numbered consecutively. Shortened forms may not be used for references cited in previous chapters; they must again be cited in full.

USE OF *IBID.*: When references to the same work follow each other *without any intervening reference,* even though they are separated by several pages, the abbreviation *ibid.* (for the Latin *ibidem,* "in the same place") is used to repeat the preceding reference. Any changes in volume and/or page number(s) must be indicated following *ibid.* However, if the reference is to the same volume and page number as the preceding reference, then nothing follows *ibid. Ibid.* may not be used to repeat *part* of a preceding reference.

Examples:

¹J. N. Hook, *The Teaching of High School English* (New York, 1950), pp. 176-177.

[*Note*: The first and therefore complete reference to the work.]

²*Ibid.*

[*Note*: Since there are no intervening references, the second mention of the work requires only *ibid.* Note that since *ibid.* is never preceded by any other word, it is always capitalized. Also since footnote # 2 refers to pp. 176-177, no page numbers need be indicated.]

³*Ibid.,* p. 39.

[*Note*: Since there have been no intervening references, *ibid.* is still correct; this time it refers to a different page. As long as there are no intervening references, *ibid.* may continue to be used.]

USE OF *OP. CIT.*: Reference to a work which has already been cited in full form, *but not in the reference immediately preceding,* should include the author's last name (but not his first name or initials unless two authors by the same last name have already been mentioned in the paper), and the abbreviation *op. cit.* (for the Latin *opere citato,* "in the work cited"). In most of these entries, *op. cit.* is followed by the page designation.

Examples:

[1]Van Wyck Brooks, *The Confident Years*: *1885-1915* (New York, 1955), p. 87.

[2]Frederick J. Hoffman, *The Twenties* (New York, 1955), pp. 189-190.

[3]Brooks, *op. cit.*, p. 81.

[*Note*: Since there was an intervening reference, *op. cit.* must be used and the new page designated.]

USE OF *LOC. CIT.*: *Loc. cit.* (for the Latin *loco citato*, "in the place cited") is used in lieu of *ibid.* when the reference is not only to the work immediately preceding but also refers to the same page. *Loc. cit.* is also used in lieu of *op. cit.* when reference is made to a work previously cited and to the same page in that work. Hence, *loc. cit.* is never followed by volume and/or page numbers. When it takes the place of *ibid.*, *loc. cit.* is capitalized.

EXAMPLES OF FOOTNOTE ENTRIES USING *IBID., OP. CIT.,* **AND** *LOC. CIT.*:

[1]Arlo Bates, *Talks on Teaching Poetry* (Boston, 1906), p. 93.

[2]J. N. Hook, *The Teaching of High School English* (New York, 1950), pp. 66-67.

[3]*Ibid.*, pp. 138-139.

[*Note*: Refers to work by J. N. Hook. If the reference had been to the same pages, *loc. cit.* would have been used.]

[4]Bates, *loc. cit.*

[*Note*: *Loc. cit.* is used since the note refers to page 93.]

[5]*Ibid.*, pp. 77-79.

[*Note*: Reference is made to the work by Bates.]

[6]*Ibid.,* p. 20.

[*Note:* Reference is again made to Bates.]

[7]Benjamin A. Heydrick, *How To Study Literature* (New York, 1901), p. v.

[8]*Loc. cit.*

[*Note*: Reference is made to the note immediately preceding. Since the reference is to the same passage, *loc. cit.* is used instead of *ibid.* Note that since no word precedes the entry, *loc. cit.* has been capitalized.]

[9]John Bates, *Poetry in Transition* (Philadelphia, 1926), pp. 101-110.

[10]Hook, *op. cit.*, p. 79.

[11]Arlo Bates, *loc. cit.*

[*Note*: Since two works have been listed by authors with the same last name, the first name of the author must be given. *Loc. cit.* refers to footnote #6, the last reference made to that work.]

[12]*Ibid.,* pp. 29-30.

[*Note*: Refers to footnote immediately preceding.]

[13]Mario Pei, *The Story of English* (New York, 1952), p. 56.

[14]John Bates, *op. cit.*, p. 5.

[15]Mario Pei, *Invitation to Linguistics: A Basic Introduction to the Science of Language* (Garden City, N. Y., 1965), pp. 48-49.

[16]Hook, *loc. cit.*

[17]Pei, *The Story of English,* p. 10.

[*Note*: Since two works have been listed by the same author, reference to either work must include the author's last name and title of the work being cited.]

SOME POINTS TO REMEMBER:

1. Footnote entries should be written when writing the first draft.

2. All entries should be checked for accuracy of information and form.

3. *Ibid.*, *loc. cit.*, and *op. cit.* must be italicized.

4. All footnote entries are single spaced. There is a double space between all entries.

5. All entries are followed by a period.

6. The same bottom margin must be maintained on all pages regardless of the number of footnotes.

7. Entries should be numbered consecutively except where the paper is divided into chapters. In that case, the first footnote entry in a chapter is "1."

8. Footnotes should be placed at the bottom of the page. Numbering and placement are greatly simplified when a word processor is used. The writer can program his computer to automatically number the notes consecutively and place them at the bottom of the appropriate pages.[2]

9. Content notes must be written in clear, concise English. When the note is long, it should be incorporated into an appendix.

The student must remember that, in part, the scholarship of his article will be judged by his documentation. The ability to refer to authorities and to substantiate his research is what lends credence to his argument.

---

[2]For more information on footnoting, see Kate L. Turabian, *A Manual for Writers of Term Papers, Theses, and Dissertations* (5th ed.: Chicago: The University of Chicago Press, 1987).

CHAPTER IX

THE BIBLIOGRAPHY

The bibliography is part of the last section of the paper and follows the text. If there are appendixes as well, the bibliography may precede or follow them, as the writer desires. With the exception of very short research papers where a bibliography may be omitted (in that case, footnote entries must include the name of the publisher, following the place of publication), a formal bibliography is a necessary part. The bibliography may be limited to only those works which the researcher found significantly relevant or include all works which were consulted in the preparation of the paper and which had any bearing whatsoever on the topic. In addition, the writer may wish to supply a listing of works which the reader may consult for a more detailed and expanded study of the general topic. Such a listing of additional sources, however, should be listed under a separate heading.

BIBLIOGRAPHICAL ORDER: The length of the bibliography will determine the basic classifications. In a comparatively short bibliography, all works will be listed under a single heading. In longer ones, where the writer consulted a number of works of many different kinds, he may choose to list these titles under separate subheadings, e.g., texts and periodicals. Conceivably, there may be even further subdivisions, e.g., public documents interviews, speeches, and reports.

Bibliographical entries are arranged alphabetically by author's last name. Where no author is listed, the work is

listed by the first word of the title exclusive of any article
(*a, an, the*), and the article is listed following the title,
e.g., "Effects of the War, The." Works with no authors
listed should not be listed under "Anonymous."

For all intents and purposes, the student's bibliography has already been arranged if he has followed the
directions for the preparation of his working bibliography,
and checked all his information against the books themselves. All he need do at this point is remove those cards
which were irrelevant and, if necessary, arrange his sources
according to type. After this, all that remains is tran-
scribing the information from the cards.

SPACING: All bibliographical entries are single spaced
with double spaces between entries. The author's last name
begins at the margin, and where the entry contains more
than one line, successive lines are indented. The same in-
dentation should be observed for all entries.

CONTENTS OF BIBLIOGRAPHICAL ENTRY: Bibliographical entries contain these facts arranged as follows:

1. The author's last name, followed by a comma; the
   first name and middle initial, followed by a period.

2. The title of the work, followed by a period. Titles
   of full-length works are italicized (underlined);
   titles of works in collections are enclosed in double
   quotation marks. All words with the exception of
   articles, prepositions, and conjunctions—unless the
   first word in the title—are capitalized.

3. The edition number, followed by a period.

4. The name of the translator, compiler, or editor
   —where pertinent—followed by a period.

5. The place of publication, followed by a colon. If
   the city is not well known, the state should also
   appear, e.g., Garden City, New York. When more
   than one place of publication is given in the book,
   generally the first one is used.

6. The name of the publisher, followed by a comma.

7. The year of publication, followed by a period. If the date of publication does not appear on the title page but has been located elsewhere, it should be enclosed within brackets. If it cannot be located, then the copyright date is given with the notation *c.* preceding it, e.g., c. 1956. Where neither date of publication nor copyright date is available, the notation *n.d.* (no date) is listed.

8. The number of pages in the work or the page numbers which contain relevant information, followed by a period. This entry is optional.

EXAMPLES OF BIBLIOGRAPHICAL ENTRIES: Compare the following bibliographical entries with the comparable footnote entries in the preceding chapter.

1. **Book—one author:**

   Potok, Chaim. *My Name Is Asher Lev.* New York: Alfred A. Knopf, 1972.

2. **Book—one author; numbered or revised edition:**

   Wiles, Kimball. *Supervision for Better Schools.* 3rd ed. Englewood Cliffs, New Jersey: Prentice-Hall, 1967.

3. **Book—one author; more than one volume:**

   Parrington, Vernon Louis. *Main Currents in American Thought.* New York: Harcourt, Brace, and Company, c. 1930. 3 vols.

4. **Book—one author; only one volume used:**

   Parrington, Vernon Louis. *Main Currents in American Thought.* New York: Harcourt, Brace, and Company, c. 1930. Vol. II.

5. **Book—two authors:**

   Masters, William H. and Virginia E. Johnson. *Human Sexual Inadequacy.* Boston: Little, Brown and Company, 1970.

[*Note*: When more than one author is listed, only the name of the first author is inverted; all other names are given in the first name-last name order.]

6. **Book—more than three authors:**

Austin, David *et al. Reading Rights for Boys: Sex Role and Development in Language Experience.* New York: Appleton-Century Crofts, 1971.

[*Note*: The words "and others" may be substituted for "*et al.*" However, the writer must use the same form as he did in the footnote entries.]

7. **Book—no author given:**

Lottery, The. London: J. Watts, [1732].

[*Note*: The article is listed following the title for ease of alphabetization.]

8. **Book—editor of a collection:**

Hollander, John, ed. *Poems of Our Moment.* New York: Pegasus, 1968.

[*Note:* If "ed." was placed within parentheses in the footnote entries, it should be done here as well.]

9. **Book—author and editor:**

Crane, Stephen. *The Red Badge of Courage.* Ed. Richard Chase. Boston: Houghton Mifflin Company, c. 1960.

10. **Book—translated into English:**

Flaubert, Gustave. *Madame Bovary.* Trans. Gerard Hopkins. New York: Dell Publishing Company, Inc., 1959.

11. **Book—no author or editor; translated:**

Anglo-Saxon Chronicle, The. Trans. G. N. Garmonsway. London: J. M. Dent and Sons, Ltd., 1953.

12. Book—article or essay by one of several contributors:

Goodman, Paul. "Growing Up Absurd — 'Human Nature' and the Organized System," *The Sense of the 60's*. Eds. Edward Quinn and Paul J. Dolan. New York: Macmillan, 1968. Pp. 3-13.

13. Book—selection in a collection by one author:

Cleaver, Eldridge. "The Allegory of the Black Eunuchs," *Soul on Ice*. New York: Dell Publishing Company, 1968. Pp. 155-175.

14. Book—same author as preceding entry:

————. "The White Race and Its Heroes," *Soul on Ice*. New York: Dell Publishing Company, 1968. Pp. 65-83.

[*Note*: The length of the horizontal line should equal that of the author's name. Where two or more works are listed by the same author, they are arranged alphabetically by the first word of the title, exclusive of the articles.]

15. Article or essay—author given:

Southern, Terry. "The Rolling Stones' U.S. Tour: Riding the Lapping Tongue," *Saturday Review*, 55:25-30. August 12, 1972.

16. Article or essay—no author given:

"South Viet Nam: Campaign of Brutality," *Time*, 100:17-18. August 21, 1972.

17. Article or essay—no author given; name supplied:

[Adams, Virginia]. "Teen-Age Sex: Letting the Pendulum Swing," *Time*, 100:34-40. August 21, 1972.

18. Article or essay—initials of author given; full name supplied:

G[unner], S[ebastian] H. "Heresy in Education," *Journal of Educational Discourse*, 15:20-31. September, 1958.

19. Article or essay—alternate entry:

Southern, Terry. "The Rolling Stones' U.S. Tour: Riding the Lapping Tongue," *Saturday Review*, LV (August 12, 1972), 25-30.

[*Note*: The writer is to use whichever form he used in the footnote entries.]

20. Articles—encyclopedias, dictionaries, etc.:

"Drama—Stories on the Stage," *Compton's Pictured Encyclopedia*. (1967), IV, 169-192.

21. Newspaper:

New York Times, September 7, 1972, Sec. 4, p. 3.

22. Newspaper—title and author given:

Taggart, Frank. "Clark Helps Revive Viet Issue," *Newsday* (Long Island), August 15, 1972, p. 5.

[*Note*: When the title of the newspaper does not include the place of publication, it should be included within parentheses following the title.]

23. Newspaper—title given; no author:

"Republicans Start in Slugging," *Newsday* (Long Island), August 15, 1972, p. 3.

24. Unpublished materials:

Teitelbaum, Harry. "A Study of Leisure-time Reading Habits of Second Year High School Students." Unpublished Master's Thesis. Brooklyn, New York: Brooklyn College, 1953.

25. Bulletin—institution or organization as author:

State University of New York at Stony Brook. *1971-72 Graduate Bulletin*. Stony Brook, New York: University Press, 1971.

26. Lecture:

> Sebastian, John. Lecture: "Naturalism in *The Red Badge of Courage.*" Community Lecture Discussion Group, September 23, 1972.

ANNOTATION: Although completely optional, the writer may wish to annotate his bibliography for the convenience of the reader. When this is done, the annotation should be single spaced and begin on the line following the bibliographical entry.

SAMPLE BIBLIOGRAPHY: The following is a sample of a bibliography at the end of a short paper. Note that the articles and periodicals are not separated from the rest of the entries. Also note that the entries are *not* numbered.

BIBLIOGRAPHY

" 'American Tragedy,' An," Literary Digest, 64:33. February 28, 1920.

Carson, William G.B. The Theatre on the Frontier, Chicago: The University of Chicago Press, 1932.

Crawford, Mary Caroline. The Romance of the American Theatre. Boston: Little, Brown, and Company, 1925.

Dickinson, Thomas H. Playwrights of the New American Theatre. New York: The Macmillan Company, 1925.

Eaton, Walter P. The American Stage of Today. Boston: Small, Maynard, and Company, 1908.

——————— . "Eugene O'Neill," Theatre Arts, 4:286-289. October, 1920.

Hornblow, Arthur. A History of the Theatre in America: From Its Beginnings to the Present Time. Philadelphia: J.B. Lippincott Company, 1919. Vol. I.

MacKaye, Percy. Epoch: The Life of Steele MacKaye, Genius
     of the Theatre, in Relation to His Times and Contempo-
     raries. New York: Boni, Liveright, 1927. Vol. I,
     pp. 333-368.

Moses, Montrose J., and John Mason Brown, eds. The Ameri-
     can Theatre as Seen by Its Critics, 1752–1934. New York:
     Norton, 1934.

Quinn, Arthur Hobson. A History of the American Drama
     from the Civil War to the Present Day. New York: F.S.
     Crofts and Company, 1937. 2 vols.

_____ , ed. Representative American Plays from 1767
     to the Present Day. New York: Appleton-Century-Crofts,
     Inc., 1953.

Reed, Perley Isaac. Realistic Presentation of American Char-
     acters in Native American Plays Prior to 1870.
     Columbus, Ohio: Ohio State University, 1918.

CHAPTER X

TABLES, GRAPHS, ILLUSTRATIONS

The purpose of tables, graphs, and illustrations is to aid in the discussion and explanation of information in the text. Hence, all illustrative materials must have a definite function and cannot just serve as "window dressing." Wherever these materials seem superfluous, they should be omitted or, if the writer feels they have some limited merit, be included in the appendix. Regardless of where they are placed, they must be clear and readily understandable.

PLACEMENT: Wherever possible, illustrative materials should immediately follow their first mention in the text. However, if the insertion of the material at that point would necessitate continuing it onto the next page, the writer may continue with the text and place the illustrative materials on the following page.

TABLES: Tables are an important adjunct in any paper which is based on collected data of a statistical nature. Whenever figures are presented to the reader, they should be tabulated for easy reference. The inclusion of a long list of figures with the text will only serve to confuse the reader. However, it must again be stressed that tables cannot be included solely for their own sake; they must serve a definite purpose of reinforcing or clarifying the text.

Numbering tables: All tables, including those in the appendix, are numbered consecutively with Arabic numerals. The table number follows the word "TABLE" typed in uppercase letters and centered above the caption. Pages containing tables are numbered in the usual manner with the page number in Arabic numerals centered at the top of the page and enclosed with dashes.

Captions: Every table must have a caption—a concise statement describing its contents—placed above the table. The caption, typed in upper case letters, is centered on the line two spaces below the table number. If the caption runs to two or more lines, it is written in inverted pyramid form. No period follows the caption. A double unbroken line is drawn the width of the table two spaces below the caption.

Each column in the table must have an appropriate and descriptive heading; because of space limitation, the heading must be concise. When the column caption consists of more than one word and the column width does not permit it to be written on a single line, the caption is arranged so that it is pleasing to the eye and its meaning clear. Captions follow the rules for capitalization in titles.

Table layout: Neatness and ease of comprehension are the guiding principles in laying out tables. However, the following rules should be adhered to:

1. A double unbroken line is placed at the top of the table, two spaces below the caption.
2. A single horizontal line is placed at the bottom of the table.
3. No vertical rules are placed at either end of the table.
4. Columns are separated with vertical rules.
5. Items within the table may be single spaced or double spaced.
6. Two-column tables contain no vertical rules.
7. Abbreviations in column captions may be used, but if they are not standard abbreviations, they must be explained in a "key" at the bottom of the table.

8. All figures are aligned by the decimal points.

9. Horizontal lines may be typed while vertical rules are inked in. However, the student may choose to ink in all lines.

Footnotes: If it is necessary to include footnotes within the table, they are placed below the bottom horizontal rule, and not at the foot of the page with other textual notes. In order to avoid confusion, lower case letters, instead of Arabic numerals are used to designate footnotes. If none of the tables has more than one footnote, an asterisk may be used, but asterisks and letters may not be used interchangeably. Footnotes are single spaced with a double space between entries.

Long tables: Tables which run to more than one page are continued on the following page with the heading "TABLE —*Continued*" centered above the double unbroken line of the table. It is not necessary to repeat the table caption. If at all possible, however, tables should not be split between pages; when a table contains too many items for it to be listed vertically, it may be arranged horizontally on a separate page. The page number, however, should appear in the usual position.

Sample tables:

TABLE 1

MAGAZINES LISTED AS FIRST CHOICE

Name of Magazine	No.	%
Life	187	25.4
Sports magazines	89	12.1
Look	61	8.3
Mechanical magazines	40	5.4
Science magazines	28	3.8
No choice indicated	331	45.0

TABLE 2

TYPES OF BOOKS PREFERRED BY HIGH SCHOOL STUDENTS (FIRST THREE CHOICES)

	Type of Book	No.	%
First Choice			
Boys	Sports	174	23.7
Girls	Novels	219	50.6
Both	Novels	292	25.0
Second Choice			
Boys	War Stories	113	15.4
Girls	Mystery	126	29.1
Both	Mystery	197	16.9
Third Choice			
Boys	War Stories	99	13.5
Girls	Comics	73	16.9
Both	Comics	147	12.6

TABLE 3

DEGREE TO WHICH STUDENTS ARE FOND OF READING

Reading Fondness	Boys		Girls		Both	
	No.	%	No.	%	No.	%
Very much	111	15.1	98	22.6	209	17.9
Quite a lot	217	29.5	164	37.9	381	32.6
A little	369	50.2	152	35.1	521	44.6
Not at all	12	1.6	7	1.6	19	1.6
Total*	709	96.4	421	97.2	1130	96.7

*Discrepancies between total responses and 100% represent the percentage who did not respond to the question.

TABLE 4

DISTRIBUTION OF AGES

Class Interval (Ages in yrs. & mos.)	Frequency
17-8 — 17-11	2
17-4 — 17- 7	11
17-0 — 17- 3	23
16-8 — 16-11	30
16-4 — 16- 7	46
16-0 — 16- 3	90
15-8 — 15-11	238
15-4 — 15- 7	291
15-0 — 15- 3	271
14-8 — 14-11	100
14-4 — 14- 7	36
14-0 — 14- 3	13
13-8 — 13-11	6
13-4 — 13- 7	1

$N = 1,158$

Mean $=$ 15 yrs. 6.7 mos.

Median $=$ 15 yrs. 5.1 mos.

Mode $=$ 15 yrs. 6.0 mos.

[*Note*: Horizontal lines could have been drawn in the above table.]

TABLE 5

SECTIONS OF DAILY NEWSPAPERS READ MOST FREQUENTLY BY HIGH SCHOOL STUDENTS

	Comics %	Sports %	Gen'l. News %	Local News %	Ads. %	Crime %	Eds. %
Boys	56.5	62.0	47.8	36.1	32.9	35.0	15.5
Girls	54.0	15.9	35.3	33.5	41.3	29.6	13.9
Both	55.6	44.9	43.2	35.1	36.0	33.0	14.9

TABLE 6

DISTRIBUTION OF IQ SCORES OF SECOND YEAR HIGH SCHOOL STUDENTS

IQ Scores	Boys (N=686)	Girls (N=404)	Both (N=1090)
	Freq.	Freq.	Freq.
160-169	1	0	1
150-159	3	1	4
140-149	12	6	18
130-139	29	8	37
120-129	52	25	77
110-119	125	60	185
100-109	171	75	246
90- 99	161	89	250
80- 89	62	78	140
70- 79	50	54	104
60- 69	17	8	25
50- 59	3	0	3
Mean	103.1	98.2	101.2
Median	102.9	97.0	100.9
Mode	105.0	95.0	95.0

GRAPHS: Graphs are actually a kind of illustration and would be included in the list of illustrations. They may be placed on separate sheets of paper or be part of the page of text. In either case, the pages are numbered consecutively. The graphs are numbered consecutively with Arabic numerals. The rules for numbering and captions are the same as for tables.

Graphs are generally line, bar, or picture graphs and will be drawn in India ink. Where several copies of the report are necessary, graphs may be reproduced by a suitable photographic process.

Graphs, as well as tables, serve a useful function when they are used as an aid to the text. They are incorporated for the convenience of the reader and should be clear, concise, and easy to comprehend. In the case of picture graphs, the writer must supply a legend.

ILLUSTRATIONS: In addition to the graphs mentioned, illustrations may consist of blueprints, pictures, diagrams, original drawings, maps, photographs, and generally anything which illustrates the text. The rules governing the use of illustrations are the same as those for tables. They should serve a definite purpose and should be placed as close to the text they illustrate as possible. The placement, numbering, writing of captions, and pagination are the same as for tables. All graphs and illustrations are included in the list of illustrations. If a paper contains a large number of graphs, the student may then make a separate list.

Not all papers will require the inclusion of tables, graphs, and/or illustrations. The student should exercise the utmost discretion when incorporating these aids, for the overuse or improper use of them will weaken rather than strengthen the overall effect of the paper. He must remember at all times that his primary purpose is to present a scholarly discussion of his research, using pictorial aids only when necessary to aid the reader's comprehension of the text.

CHAPTER XI

THE FINAL MANUSCRIPT

Before the student is ready to type his final manuscript, he will have written his first draft of the complete paper including footnotes, table of contents, list of tables, bibliography, and appendixes. Furthermore, he will have edited these drafts (the plural is used because it is assumed that there were several revisions—especially for style—which necessitated the rewriting of the first or "rough" draft either in part or completely) for any structural, mechanical, or content errors. In addition, he will have supplied a title which is concise and descriptive of the contents; and he will have checked his footnotes, bibliography, illustrations, and all other reference notes for accuracy. Once all this has been done, the student is ready to prepare the final manuscript which, in some instances, may be written in longhand, but most often must be typed by the writer or submitted to a professional typist. Regardless of which method is employed, the writer must hold himself responsible for any and all errors in the final manuscript.

GENERAL TYPING DIRECTIONS: All dissertations and theses, and most research papers, must be typed. It is the rare instructor who will accept handwritten papers. If the student is a good enough typist, he should type his own papers, for the use of a professional typist can be costly. (Typists charge per page, plus an additional charge for each carbon copy. Whether a professional types the paper, or whether the student does so himself, he must be sure he has a carbon copy made.) However, the student should remember that there is no such thing as a typographical error in the final manuscript; all errors are the writer's. A word processor will make copyreading and proofreading much simpler.

Type of paper: The student should use a good grade of bond paper. Erasable bond is highly recommended, for it will permit use of a pencil eraser without leaving smudges. The paper must be white and unlined.

Typewriter: The typewriter should be in good working order. Keys should be cleaned periodically during the typing of the manuscript. The ribbon should retain a sufficient amount of ink for a uniformly clear imprint. When the subject matter requires the use of special characters, e.g., mathematical symbols, the writer must either use a typewriter containing these characters or have the paper typed professionally. These characters should not be inked in. A word processor and good-quality printer will simplify the entire process and give the writer a professional-looking manuscript. The writer, though, should not engage in the creative use of different fonts.

Margins: Margins on all four sides of the paper should be equal. Since the paper will be stapled or bound on the left, the space taken up by the binding must be added to that margin. The top and bottom margins must be constant. On footnoted pages where the text ends before the bottom margin, the entry is placed so that the bottom margin is uniform. Careful planning will minimize the irregularity of the right-hand margin. Although word processors will enable the writer to justify the right margin, it is not recommended for research papers.

Spacing: All typed manuscript, with the exception of footnotes, bibliographical entries, and quotations set off from the text, is double spaced. Other rules to be followed are:

1. All chapters and other divisions begin on a new page regardless of how much space is left on the preceding page.

2. On title pages of chapters and other divisions, the chapter number (e.g., CHAPTER III) is centered on the line, eight spaces from the top edge of the paper.

3. On all other pages, the page number is centered on the line (enclosed in dashes) two spaces from the top edge of the paper.

4. Following the chapter number, the title of the chapter is centered on the line two spaces below the chapter designation.

5. Three spaces below the chapter title, the text is begun.

6. On pages other than title pages, the text begins eight spaces from the top edge of the paper (six spaces below the page number).

7. All paragraphs should be indented seven spaces from the margin.

8. All footnote entries are to be single spaced with double spaces between the entries.

9. All quotations set off from the text and indented left and right are single spaced.

10. All bibliographical entries are single spaced with double spaces between the entries.

Footnotes: All footnotes should appear at the bottom of the page. This often presents a problem in keeping proper bottom margins. The student will find it helpful to make a light pencil guide mark at the left bottom edge of the paper as he inserts it in his typewriter. When that line appears, he knows the line he is currently typing must be his last. As he indicates a footnote number in the text on the page, he should stop and, depending on the length of the entry, move that pencil mark up. Here again, the word processor will simplify this task by automatically numbering the footnotes and placing them at the bottom of the appropriate pages.

When a footnote entry is so long that it must be continued on the following page, the entry should be begun immediately following the place where it is referred to in the text and continued until the bottom margin. The remainder of the note is then continued on the next page in the footnote area (below the horizontal line) preceding any footnotes for that page. The continuation should *not* be indicated by any such statements as "continued on next page," or "continued." Only one footnote entry should appear on any one line.

Half-title page: Major divisions (e.g., parts, sections, appendixes) are generally introduced by a half-title page—a sheet which contains the part number and title centered on the page and typed in upper-case letters throughout. Half-title pages are numbered with the rest of the paper but the page number is *not* placed on the page.

Proofreading: The final manuscript must be proofread very carefully. This means that the writer will read the typed manuscript and the draft simultaneously, making certain that there are no differences between the two. Minor errors should be corrected by erasing carefully and typing in the corrections. However, where there are several errors, the entire page should be re-typed.

With the possible exception of illustrations and brackets, everything in a typed manuscript must be typed.

GENERAL DIRECTIONS FOR HANDWRITTEN MANU-SCRIPTS: To be sure, all theses and dissertations must be typed, but some instructors will not object when research papers for courses are submitted in handwritten form. However, if the student's penmanship tends to be sloppy or illegible, he should have his paper typed.

Type of paper: The student should use white, lined paper, with a ruled left-hand margin. Wide-spaced paper should be used.

Margins: The wide top margin and the ruled left margin are sufficient. Right-hand margin should be one inch and the bottom margin should be the last one and one-half spaces.

Spacing: Although writing on every other line is recommended, the student may write on every line, skipping a line between paragraphs. He is to write on one side of the paper only. Other rules to be followed are:

1. All chapters and other divisions begin on a new page regardless of how much space is left on the preceding page.

2. On title pages of chapters and other divisions, the chapter number with the word *chapter* is centered within the first space of the page. The chapter title is placed on the line immediately below the chapter designation. Titles and the word *chapter* are written in upper-lower case.

3. One space is skipped between the chapter title and the first line of the chapter.

4. On all other pages, the text begins within the first space.

5. On title pages, the page number is centered on the line, enclosed with dashes, within the last full space on the page. On all other pages, the number, enclosed with dashes, is centered near the top of the top margin.

6. All paragraphs should be indented approximately one inch from the margin.

7. All footnote entries appear at the bottom of the page. A solid horizontal line, extending from the left hand margin to the right, is drawn one space below the last line of the text. Entries are single spaced with a line skipped between entries.

8. All other rules are the same as for typed manuscript.

Sample page:

> *Chapter VI*
> *The Newer Approaches*
>
> *Although there have been a*
> *variety of improvements in*
>
> ---
>
> *"a little improvement"[6] is not*
>
> [6] *John Marks, Criticism in America*
> *(New York, 1968), p. 28.*
>
> *— 19 —*

Ink: All handwritten papers must be written in black, blue, or blue-black ink. All drawings and illustrations should be done in India ink.

COLLATING: Once the paper has been carefully proofread, it is ready to be collated. The student should be sure to place a blank sheet following the title page and another blank sheet after the last page of the paper. The paper should then be fastened along the left-hand margin with two or, at the most, three staples. If he so desires, he may enclose the manuscript in a plain manila or thesis folder. Where a folder is used, the title of the paper and the writer's name should appear on the cover.

The research project is now complete, the paper is written, and, in all probability, the student has found that it was a truly rewarding experience which not only made him keenly aware of a new aspect in the field but also whetted his appetite for further research.

CHAPTER XII

THE SHORTER THEME

It is generally assumed that before one undertakes to write a research paper, he has mastered the art of writing the shorter theme or the essay. Here again it must be stressed that, theoretically at least, the student is not writing solely to fulfill a course requirement; such themes often tend to be rather sterile. It is hoped that he is writing because he has something to say, something that he feels he must communicate. And communication is the only valid reason for writing. In this sense, the writer is an artist who chooses pen and paper rather than canvas and paint with which to express his thoughts and ideas. Although he may choose various modes of written expression —poem, short story, play, mood piece— this chapter will focus on the expository essay, that form of written expression that the student will probably use most often during his school years.

Topic limitation. — Topic selection should not present a major problem. At best, the topic has been in the student's mind for a long time, and he is most anxious to get his ideas and thoughts on paper so that others can share his thinking; or, at worst, the topic has been assigned him by his instructor. The main problem, however, that he will confront is how to limit the topic, but before he can do that, there are several factors he must consider.

Purpose or objective:

Before he begins to write —or outline his paper, for that matter —the student must be certain of his purpose or objective: Does he simply want *to inform* his readers, or does he want *to persuade* or *convince* them to think along certain lines? Perhaps his objective is *to move-to-action*, to get his readers to follow a course, or perhaps his aim is simply *to entertain?* Certainly, these aims are not mutually exclusive, and it is conceivable that an effective theme may incorporate all of these objectives. However, one of these objectives should be dominant for it will determine the overall organization, diction, and tone of the theme. For example, the move-to-action theme must be much more forceful and dynamic than the persuasive theme, for although both will attempt to convince the reader, the former must get him to act whereas the latter is content with the reader's passive acceptance of an idea.

Audience:

To be certain, the audience —the readers for whom the writer is writing— may help to determine the writer's objective. But the audience serves a much more important function: it will determine the writer's level of language, his diction, the degree of difficulty of the subject matter, the intensity and extensity of the theme. The writer must ascertain the age of his audience, its educational and/or intellectual level, its knowledgeability of the subject matter, its interests, its prejudices. Each of these will affect not only his topic limitation but his overall approach as well.

Time limitation:

The amount of time the student is given to write his paper is also extremely important. A paper which must be produced within the confines of a fifty-minute class period can not hope to be as extensive —or intensive— as a paper which can be worked on for several days. The same applies to word limitation, for these both are restrictive measures which more so than any other factors demand topic limitation.

Once the student is aware of all the aforementioned factors, he is ready to limit his topic, keeping uppermost in his mind that he is obligated to say something useful and not just fill up space with words. Therefore, if he wants to write about women's lib, he cannot hope to deal with the subject in its entirety within the limitation of a 1000-word paper; he must limit his topic. Depending upon his audience and his own knowledge of the subject, he might limit the topic to "the equality of women in the professions," or limit it further to "the equality of women in law." The important factor is that the limitation will permit him to say something in depth, something that will not be a waste of the reader's time.

Outlining.—Once the student has decided on his topic limitation, his objective, and collected all of his information, he is ready to begin his outline. The outline is perhaps the most essential step in the writing process for it permits him to see at a glance whether the paper will be unified.

The *thesis statement,* or the statement of theme, is the focal point of the outline for it states concisely the writer's objective. It is important, therefore, that the writer give careful thought to writing this statement, revising it as often as necessary until he is certain that it encompasses his aim for the paper. Under no condition is he to begin outlining before he has set down his thesis statement and is certain that it is an accurate statement of his aim.

The thesis statement should be phrased as a statement and not as a question. If the topic is "the equality of women in law," he might formulate his statement as follows: *Thesis statement: In law, more so than in any other profession, women have equal opportunities with men.* This statement will now set the tone for his paper. The student must now proceed to prove this thesis. However, before he can begin to outline, he must know what basic method of development he will use.

As in paragraph development (which is discussed later in this chapter), themes should be developed either by instances and examples, comparison and/or contrast, cause and effect, definition, anecdote, or steps in a process. Although these methods of development are not mutually exclusive, one of them should dominate. It is that dominant method which will affect the outline. For example, if the basic method is instances and examples, then the outline must contain instances and/or examples which will effectively substantiate the thesis. If, on the other hand, the method is anecdote, then the outline must contain a detailed occurrence which will, through the telling of the anecdote, substantiate the thesis.

In outlining, the student has two forms from which he can choose: the Harvard (formal) outline and the informal outline. The former is an extremely flexible format which can be employed as readily for a short theme or for a book whereas the latter can be employed only for the short theme.

The Harvard outline follows a rigid format: Roman numerals indicate major divisions (in the longer paper, they can indicate parts of the paper; in the shorter paper, paragraphs); upper case letters indicate sub-divisions; Arabic numerals further sub-divisions. For example:

I.

II.

III.

   A.
   B.
   C.

     1.
     2.

      a.
      b.
      c.
      d.

          (1)
          (2)

               (a)
               (b)

IV.

The indention must be exactly as above. Furthermore, items should be expressed in parallel form, i.e., if item I. is a prepositional phrase, then all Roman numeral items must be prepositional phrases; if A. is an infinitive, then all upper-case items under the same Roman numeral must be infinitives. Also, there must be at least two subtopics (or none), for sub-topics are sub-divisions, and no item can be divided into fewer than two parts.

Although the formal outline may, at first glance, seem too formal and stiff, it is a form that the student would do well to master, for it will permit him to see at a glance whether he is developing his thesis or not.

The informal outline is just that — extremely informal. Here all the student does is jot down in phrase form all those items which he thinks will help him to prove his thesis. After he has completed the listing, he ascertains whether each item will help him to prove the thesis. If not, the item is. eliminated. The remaining items are then arranged in logical order.

Regardless of which type of outline the student uses, he must recognize that once the outline has been completed, he must follow it without any deviation. Should he feel compelled, while writing the paper, to deviate, he can do so only if he revises the outline in its entirety. An outline which is not scrupulously followed serves no useful purpose whatsoever.

Paragraphing. — Before dealing with the actual writing of the theme, it might be well to digress at this point to discuss paragraph development and organization, for the paragraph is a multi-paragraphed theme in miniature where each paragraph is comparable to each sentence in the paragraph.

The expository paragraph consists of the development of a single idea through a series of related sentences. The idea is introduced by a topic sentence which sets forth the main idea of the paragraph; it is developed through a series of related sentences which prove the topic statement; and it is ended with a concluding sentence. The effective paragraph must be unified and coherent. Let us look at each of these characteristics individually.

Topic sentence:

The topic sentence encompasses the gist of the paragraph and sets its tone. As such, it usually comes at the beginning of the paragraph, although it could come in the middle or at the end. There are two types of topic sentences that the writer can employ: the direct statement and the indirect. For example:

Direct: Student activism has contributed substantially to the elimination of formal undergraduate requirements. In developing this paragraph, the writer must show specifically *how* student activism has contributed to the elimination of formal undergraduate requirements.

Indirect: Recently I had an interesting chat with an educator friend of mine concerning the future of television. This paragraph will focus on the future of educational television. The reference to "educator friend of mine" implied the limitation.

Regardless of which type of topic sentence is employed, it must be vivid, stimulating, and exciting, for it will determine whether or not the reader reads the rest of the paragraph. The writer must always remember that he is striving to retain the reader's attention and interest. The reader, unlike the listener who remains throughout the speech because common courtesy demands it, is free to stop reading at any time, and once he stops reading the selection, there is nothing the writer can do to regain his attention.

Methods of paragraph development:

It is in the body of the paragraph where the writer *proves* his topic sentence. If the development is weak or incomplete, then the writer has failed to make his point. It is, therefore, essential that the paragraph is adequately developed. A two or three sentence paragraph is comparable to a very skimpy sandwich—very unsatisfying. Although the bottom slice of bread, like the topic sentence, supports the sandwich meats, it is the sandwich meats that make the sandwich worthwhile. So it is with the paragraph. The *tastiness* of the paragraph is, in part, determined by the method of development the writer uses.

1. *Instances and/or examples.*—In the paragraph of instances and examples (instances are actual occurrences; examples are fictitious events) the writer will select those instances or examples which will *best* substantiate his topic sentence. He must be careful not to use too few instances, leaving the reader unconvinced, nor to use too many, leaving the reader bored.

Sample paragraph — instances and/or examples:

Live television has many hazards. On a recent news broadcast, for instance, the audience was shown film clips of a beauty pageant as the newscaster introduced scenes from the Democratic convention. In another broadcast, the announcer had a coughing fit just as he was lighting the cigarette which he was advertising. And perhaps most noteworthy of all was the case of the famed chanteuse whose strap broke just as she was reaching for that high note. Yes, live television certainly has its hazards.

2. *Comparison and/or contrast.*—Most significant here is that the topic sentence must state or imply that a comparison (similarities of two or more items) or contrast (differences) will be made. At no time can the writer

begin discussing Macbeth and then later in the paragraph discuss Hamlet, unless he has so stated in the topic sentence. Such a paragraph will lack unity.

There are two ways in which the paragraph of comparison and/or contrast can be developed. In the first instance, the writer will state all he has to say about Macbeth and then state all the comparable items about Hamlet. In the second instance, he will follow each statement about Macbeth with a comparable statement about Hamlet. This could be illustrated as follows:

Topic sentence —   Macbeth and Hamlet

Development —   { Macbeth; Macbeth; Macbeth
                        { Hamlet; Hamlet; Hamlet

Concluding sentence — Macbeth and Hamlet

or:

Topic sentence —   Macbeth and Hamlet

Development —   { Macbeth; Hamlet
                       { Macbeth; Hamlet
                       { Macbeth; Hamlet

Concluding sentence — Macbeth and Hamlet

Sample paragraph — comparison and/or contrast:

Writing is very similar to painting. Both the artist and the writer have something that they feel an unrelenting urge to express; something that they must communicate. The artist makes use of his canvas, his paints, and his brushes. The writer employs his paper, his words, and his pen. Whereas the artist makes effective use of colors and brush strokes so does the writer through his careful use of words and syntax. Although the finished product is different, both artist and writer have expressed their feelings and, hopefully, communicated them to others.

3. *Cause and effect.*—Depending on the content, the paragraph of cause and effect can consist of a topic sentence which is a statement of cause followed by a series

of sentences which indicate the effects of said cause, or a topic sentence which is a statement of the effect (the end result) of several causes. In a sense, this method of paragraph development is nothing more than a paragraph of instances and examples where the instances are either causes or effects.

4. *Definition.*—Occasionally, a writer needs to define a term or concept within a longer paper. As a rule, such a term would be an abstract rather than a concrete term, for if the definition can readily be found in the dictionary, there is little need for the writer to devote a paragraph defining it. Hence, the paragraph of definition should never begin with "According to the dictionary...."

The term can be defined in several different ways. One way is to compare or contrast it to another item or concept. Another way is to define it through instances or examples. A third way is by an anecdote which illustrates the concept. It is even conceivable to use a combination of these methods.

5. *Anecdote.*—An anecdote is little more than a sustained instance or example. The paragraph of anecdote basically employs the narrative technique wherein the writer recalls an occurrence (or fabricates one) which will substantiate his topic statement. It is, incidentally, this method of development which lends itself most readily to having the topic sentence appear at the end of the paragraph.

Sample paragraph — anecdote:

Contrary to popular belief, not all teachers are insensitive to their students' needs. I well remember an incident that happened many years ago in an old dilapidated elementary school in Brooklyn. Having arrived from Europe only days before and being unable to speak any English, I was enrolled in school, but in first grade rather than in the fourth where I belonged. I felt completely ill at ease: the kids stared at me, this gangling kid who was too big for the seat and who could speak only German. However, the teacher's warm smile, her attempts to communicate with me in her high school German, her spending her lunch hour and the recess period with me soon made me feel comfortable in these new surroundings. It was her warmth and sensitivity which made me want to keep going to school and learn the language and the customs of this new country.

6. *Steps-in-a-process.*—Whereas the preceding paragraphs are generally developed logically, either in ascending or descending order of importance, the paragraph of steps-in-a-process is developed chronologically. This paragraph is geared primarily to explaining the step-by-step procedure to be followed in fulfilling any given task. The main objective of the writer is to be sure that anyone reading the paragraph will be able to accomplish the task described without any difficulty.

Sample paragraph — steps-in-a-process:

Almost anyone can learn how to boil water. First of all, supply yourself with the following materials: a metal container approximately six inches deep and five inches in diameter, preferably with a handle; water; a stove or hot plate; and matches or an electric outlet. Once you have assembled all these materials, you are ready for step two. Take the metal container in hand and proceed to the water supply, filling the pot within one inch of the rim. After turning off the water supply, proceed to the stove and place the container on the burner, being careful not to spill the water. Now light the burner so that the temperature will reach 450 degrees. Watch the water carefully and note when it begins to bubble. As soon as the water bubbles furiously, the water is boiled. At this time, turn off the supply of heat; you have just boiled water.

7. *Combination.*—None of these methods are mutually exclusive and, hence, they can be used in a combination. For example, the paragraph of comparison could employ

instances; the paragraph of definition could employ contrasts and instances. It is possible, although not probable, that a paragraph could combine all methods here discussed.

Concluding sentence:

Needless to say, each paragraph must have a concluding sentence, a sentence which lets the reader know that the writer has finished. At no time, however, should that sentence begin with "in conclusion," for that would be an admission of ineffectiveness of the ending. The ending should be a logical conclusion which says, in essence, to the reader: Look, I have just proven my topic statement.

Unity and coherence:

Unity and coherence are essential in paragraph development. Unity is achieved by ascertaining that each sentence within the paragraph is relevant to the topic sentence; that is that each sentence is a *further* development and substantiation of the topic sentence. Coherence is the logical connection of the sentences to each other. Coherence can be achieved through a variety of techniques. (See page 43).

To assure unity and coherence in the paragraph, the writer should ask himself whether each sentence is relevant to the topic statement and whether it adds something to that which has already been said. If the answer is yes for each sentence in the paragraph, then the paragraph is unified. In addition, he should also ask himself if each sentence logically follows that which precedes it and if it is properly joined to the thought which follows. If the answer is yes, then the paragraph is coherent.

The writer might want to think of his paragraph as being comparable to a train. The locomotive is the topic sentence which gives the train (paragraph) its direction. Each car is a sentence which must belong with the rest of the train for it must go where the locomotive goes, and each car must be properly coupled to the car before and after it. And, finally, the caboose is the concluding sentence which indicates that it is the last car in the train.

Introductory paragraph. — The introductory paragraph is, perhaps, the most important part of the entire theme and deservant of the greatest effort. It is this paragraph which will determine whether the reader will read the essay. A dull, boring opening, such as "In this paper I will discuss . . .," will prompt the reader to turn to another selection immediately. The introduction must be stimulating, vivid, alive, causing the reader to be anxious to read on. In addition, of course, this paragraph should contain the essence of the thesis, an implication of the method of development, and set the tone of the paper. On a purely mechanical level, each developmental sentence in the introductory paragraph could serve as a topic sentence for each paragraph within the theme.

Development — the body of the paper. — Once the reader's appetite has been whetted by the introductory paragraph, the writer must now strive to retain the reader's interest with every single paragraph. He must always keep uppermost in his mind that the reader is fickle, that he can stop reading at anytime he becomes bored, and there is absolutely no way that the writer can bring him back to the paper. The writer should keep asking himself: What is so good about my paper that the reader will prefer reading it to all the others available to him?

The outline and the method of development will determine the body of the paper. The paper of comparison and/or contrast will develop its thesis by comparing and/or contrasting two characters, ideas, or events. To be certain, such a method of development does not imply that every paragraph within the paper will be one of comparison and/or contrast. It is very likely that some paragraphs could be developed by instances and examples, some by cause and effect, some by anecdote, and some by comparison.

Again, on a purely mechanical level, each paragraph in the theme could be the development of a sentence in the introductory paragraph:

Introductory paragraph: Topic sentence
                          Sentence 1
                          Sentence 2
                          Sentence 3
                          Sentence 4
                          Concluding sentence

Development:

  Paragraph 1: Topic sentence = sentence 1
               Sentence A
               Sentence B
               Sentence C
               Concluding sentence

  Paragraph 2: Topic sentence = sentence 2
               Sentence D
               Sentence E
               Sentence F
               Sentence G
               Concluding sentence

  Paragraph 3: Topic sentence = sentence 3

  Paragraph 4: Topic sentence = sentence 4

It should be remembered, however, that such a purely mechanical method of development could create a very dull and stilted paper.

Concluding paragraph. — The concluding paragraph lets the reader know in no uncertain terms that the argument has been presented in its entirety and that the writer is finished. The well-organized argument comes to its conclusion logically and naturally. If the writer finds himself having to say "in conclusion" or "to sum up," or any other comparable phrase, he is, in fact, suggesting that his ending is weak. Although a re-phrasing of the introductory paragraph is better than no ending at all, the test of the good ending is simple: if it were at the bottom of the page, would the reader be tempted to turn to the next page for the continuation. If no, then the ending was strong, forceful, and final. The student must remember that the ending is the last thought that he leaves with his reader.

Unity and coherence. — The concepts of unity and coherence discussed for the paragraph apply here as well. Just as each paragraph must have unity, so must the theme as a whole. The writer must be positive that each paragraph is a further development of the thesis stated in the introduction. He must also be certain that there is proper transition from one paragraph to the next, that paragraphs follow each other in logical sequence, that the point of view has been maintained, and that tangential and irrelevant ideas have not been introduced.[3] To achieve all this may require *several* drafts before he is ready to write his final paper. Good writing is not accidental nor is it easy; it is a time consuming, difficult undertaking, but one which, when well done, can be highly rewarding, for what greater thrill can there be than to communicate one's ideas, thoughts, or feelings to others?

Title. — Although the title of the paper may be supplied last, it is an integral and important part of the paper. It entices the reader to choose to read the paper; it either states or implies the content; and it sets the tone. Without the title the paper is incomplete. Therefore, it becomes imperative that the writer give careful consideration to the selection of an appropriate title, one which is concise, interest-arousing, and holds the promise of great things to come.

---

[3]For a detailed discussion on coherence and unity, point of view, and some aspects of style, see pp. 43-50.

The well written theme is one that the writer is proud of. It is a theme that he will not be ashamed to have published under his name or have read by his peers. If he is writing only to fulfill course requirements or for his instructor whom he considers an impersonal reading machine, it is better that he not write at all.

APPENDIX I

1. Sample Notecard—summary:

Stephen Crane - Background ⑥

    Received military instruction at his prep school (Cloverack); he excelled in it.

    Became acquainted with a General Van Patten. Stories told by General at the school may be similar to those of Henry F. in <u>RBOC</u>.

                      pp. 1-2

---

2. Sample Notecard—combination paraphrase and direct quotation:

Naturalism in RBOC - Animal Behavior ③

    Henry F. had no control over his actions; ". . . he could not flee, no more than a little finger can commit a revolution from a hand."   p.31

    A soldier who came from the lines before the enemy advanced was stopped and slapped repeatedly by the lt. The soldier ". . . stared with sheep-like eyes" and went back to the battle like ". . . a driven animal."

                      p. 33

---

3. Sample Notecard—direct quotation with personal comment:

> *Definition of Naturalism* ②
>
>   "Naturalism has implications that are pessimistic, irrationalist, and amoral since its technique is to break down into a shimmering flow of experience the three dimensions that symbolized rationality and religious and social order in traditional art."   *p. xii*
>
>   [possible use as concluding part of paper.]

4. Sample Notecard—outline form:

> *Naturalism in RBOC – Animal Behavior* ③
>
>   Following are examples of animalistic behavior in *RBOC*:
>
>   1. like a proverbial chicken — *p. 38*
>   2. Henry, like "a pestered animal," "a cow carried by dogs." — *p. 32*
>   3. Armies fought "panther fashion." *p. 44*
>   4. Rage equal to that of "a driven beast." — *p. 33*
>   5. They viewed battle with the "...orbs of a jaded horse." — *p. 37*

SAMPLE RESEARCH PAPER
MLA STYLE

LITERATURE AND BIOGRAPHY

By Harry Teitelbaum

English-education 311.13

Hofstra University
January 15, 1993

[This sample research paper uses the University of Chicago style since it is the more difficult. Sample pages 6 and 7 using the MLA style can be found following the bibliography.]

PREFACE

I have been troubled for years with the very common practice in English
literature texts, especially anthologies used in the secondary schools, of giving
detailed biographical and social background of the writer and the work before
the student has even had the opportunity of reading the selection. Some of
these texts, particularly in the realm of poetry, will go as far as to "suggest" the
"true" interpretation of the poem. What happens so often, of course, is that
the student will simply re-state the editor's point of view rather than attempt
to formulate one of his own. Hence, both the teacher and the student are never
quite certain whether the student has obtained anything from the work itself.

To an extent this also holds true for the biographical information supplied.
If the student is told before reading that the author tends to write about certain
subjects or tends to take a certain point of view, the reader's own interpretation
will, no doubt, be strongly influenced, either consciously or subconsciously.
His interpretation will become prejudiced in favor of the one he has read, especially since the average high school student lacks confidence in his interpretive
ability to begin with.

The problem, then, is what to do about it. For one, it is extremely difficult to ask the student to ignore what precedes the selection, for even when the
biographical information appears at the end of the text, the student is quick to
realize that this presents a "clue" to him which will take the burden of interpretation off his shoulders. For two, trained as so many of us have been in the bio-
graphical-critical and historical-critical approach, we will tend to supply the student with this background as motivation for reading the literary work. In order
to see what can be done about this, I was interested in determining the thinking
of the critics on this subject.

Aside from studying the biography of an author as an entity in itself without relating the biographical aspects to his writing, there seem to be two approaches to literature and biography. One is the use of the poem[1] as a clue to the author's life, and the second is the use of the known facts of the author's life as an aid in the interpretation of the poem.

Insofar as I am concerned, the discussion of the first approach, i.e., that the poem is a source of the author's biography, is purely academic, especially in those instances where no biographical proof exists outside of the poem. The analysis, for example, of Shakespeare's works by critics who have argued that, based on his works, Shakespeare must have been a lawyer, a soldier, a teacher, a farmer, etc., is pure academic guesswork. The critic who feels that the author must have based everything on personal experience strikes me as being somewhat naive. Ellen Terry, according to Wellek and Warren, gave the crushing reply to all this literary detective work when she argued that, by the same criteria, Shakespeare must have been a woman.[2]

Yet this approach was and is being used. Robert Gittlings, in John Keats: The Living Year (1954), presents some new information about the circumstances in which Keats produced the poems he wrote between September 1818 and September 1819. He suggests that the "Bright Star" sonnet was originally written not to Fanny Brawne but to Mrs. Isabella Jones.[3] Although this may alter our view of Keats' life and his mind, it will not alter our view of his poetry. Similar kinds of literary-biographical detective work was carried out by others as well, among them Miss Wade, in her Life of Traherne, Virginia Moore in Eager Death of Emily Bronte, and numerous others in the many works about the lives of the Brontes, Shakespeare, Gray, Donne, Burns, and others.

Perhaps the most fascinating of all these works is Frank Harris' The Man

---

[1] The term poem in this paper refers to all literary works.

[2] Rene Wellek and Austin Warren, Theory of Literature (New York, 1942), p. 67, citing Ellen Terry.

[3] David Daiches, Critical Approaches to Literature (Englewood Cliffs, N.J., 1956), p. 338.

- 2 -

Shakespeare and His Tragic Life-Story. Here Harris "proves" that Shakespeare
". . . painted himself at full-length, not once, but twenty times, at as many different periods of his life."[4] And an interesting account of Shakespeare's life it is, but how much truth there is in this biographical account is highly doubtful. Harris seems to work under the complete assumption, which to me is unacceptable, that the author bases everything on personal experience.

In answer to E.M.W. Tillyard's Milton (1930), where he treats Paradise Lost as the record of the poet's state of mind during the period when he wrote it, C.S. Lewis counters that Paradise Lost was not about Milton's state of mind, but about Satan, Adam and Eve, the fall of Man, and similar subjects. Lewis cannot accept the concept that to read poetry well is to have a true idea of the poet, while to read poetry poorly is to have a false idea of him. He feels that when we read poetry as "poetry should be read," we have before us no representation which claims to be the poet, and frequently no representation of " . . . a man, a character, or a personality at all."[5]

Using the Prelude as an example, Lewis argues that if we take Wordsworth's poem as a whole, the appreciation of it as poetry does not include the knowledge that it is autobiographical. "A process of human development, that is, a particular man growing up, is presented to us; that this man is, or is intendend to be, Wordsworth himself, we learn from literary history - - unless we are so simple as to suppose that the use of the first person settles the question."[6] We do not know whether the story of the sonnets was Shakespeare's own story (Mr. Harris to the contrary); we do not know whether Milton really grieved for the death of Mr. King; and if we know that Shelley really met Keats, we do not know it " . . . in and by appreciating Adonais."[7]

---

[4]Frank Harris, The Man Shakespeare and His Tragic Life-Story (New York, 1909), p. x.

[5]C.S. Lewis, "The Personal Heresy in Criticism," Essays and Studies by Members of the English Association, collected by D. Nichol Smith (Oxford, 1934), XIX, 9.

[6]Ibid., p. 13.

[7]Loc. cit.

- 3 -

Wellek and Warren too are in agreement with this point of view when they state that it is not self-evident that a writer needs to be in a tragic mood to write tragedies or that he writes comedies when he feels pleased with life. There is simply no proof for the sorrows of Shakespeare. He cannot be made responsible for the views of Timon or Macbeth on life. "The relationship between the private life and the work is not a simple relationship of cause and effect."[8]

Lewis tends to explain away, in part, the personal dogma by recognizing that this personal view offers obvious advantages. Very few care for beauty; but anyone can be interested in gossip. "To such people any excuse for shutting up the terrible books with all the lines and lines of verse in them and getting down to the snug or piquant details of human life, will always be welcome."[9] But, yet, he feels that there is a deeper reason than this:

> The personal dogma springs from an inability which most moderns feel to make up their minds between two alternatives. A materialist, and a spiritual, theory of the universe are both equally fatal to it; but in the coming and going of the mind between the two it finds its opportunity. For the typical modern critic is usually a half-hearted materialist. He accepts, or thinks he accepts, that picture of the world which popularized science gives him. He thinks that everything except the buzzing electrons is subjective fancy; and he therefore believes that all poetry must come out of the poet's head and express (of course) his pure, uncontaminated, undivided "personality," because outside of the poet's head there is nothing but the interplay of blind forces. But he forgets that if materialism is true, there is nothing else inside the poet's head either. For a consistent materialism, the poetless poetry . . . and the most seemingly self-expressive "human document," are equally accidental results of the impersonal and irrational causes. And if this is so, if the sensation . . . which we call "enjoying poetry" in no case betokens that we are really in the presence of purpose and spirituality, then there is no foothold left for the personal heresy.[10]

Although I am more inclined to agree with this point of view, there is something to be said for Tillyard's rebuttal to Lewis wherein he contends that although the poet may, as T.S. Eliot claims, surrender himself wholly to the work to be done, the paradox consists that the poet, as a result of self-surrender, often produces the most personal and characteristic work. "The more the poet experiences this abandonment of personality," Tillyard states, "the more likely is the reader to hail the poet's charac-

---

[8]Wellek, op. cit., p. 65.

[9]Lewis, op. cit., p. 27.

[10]Ibid., pp. 27-28.

- 4 -

teristic, unmistakable self . . . Nor will it make the poet any less personal, if he carefully avoids every vestige of private emotion, if he seeks the utmost justification. On
the contrary, . . . [this] will express all the more clearly . . . the characteristic lines
of the poet's mental pattern."[11]

Of course, insofar as I can see, this does not negate the basic problem of the
critic "reading into" the poem. For an attempt to determine the mental processes
and personal experiences of the poet based solely on the poem is still a dangerous
and highly questionable, albeit interesting, undertaking.

The strongest argument I have come across favoring the use of poems as materials for biography is that of Leslie A. Fiedler who feels that the anti-biographical arguments were in reaction to Romantic subjectivity. In his article, "Archetype and
Signature: A Study of the Relationship between Biography and Poetry," Fiedler
presents the argument that anti-biographists felt that the Romantic approach at-
tempted to prove that the work of art was

> . . . nothing but the personality of the Genius behind it or the sum total of its
> genetic factors . . . The antibiographists offered . . . the "intrinsic" approach,
> which turned out . . . to be another nothing but under its show of righteous
> indignation, namely, the contention that a poem was nothing but "words,"
> and its analysis therefore properly nothing but a study of syntax and seman-
> tics. Any attempt to illuminate a poem by reference to its author's life came,
> therefore, to be regarded with horror.[12]

He is further opposed to the concept of "A poem should not mean but be."
Also he objects to the argument that the poem is self-contained and nothing exists
outside of it, (e.g., How long was Hamlet in Wittenberg?).

These, then, are the major arguments presented for and against the use of the
poem as a biographical source. Interesting though this literary detective work may
be, it still is nothing more than an academic exercise which will never offer any conclusive proof. For I am in complete agreement with Wellek and Warren when they
point out that "the work of art is not a document for biography."[13]

---

[11] E.M.W. Tillyard, "The Personal Heresy in Criticism: A Rejoinder," Essays
and Studies by Members of the English Association, collected by George Cookson
(Oxford, 1935), XX, 13-14.

[12] Leslie A. Fiedler, "Archetype and Signature: A Study of the Relationship
between Biography and Poetry," Sewanee Review, 60:254, 1952.

[13] Wellek, op. cit., p. 67.

- 5 -

The second approach to literature - - the use of the known facts of the author's life as an aid in the interpretation of the poem - - perhaps has greater validity, for here one may find information which may prove to be useful for a better understanding of the literary work. How valid, though, this approach is remains to be seen, for here, too, critics seem to stand divided.

Fiedler again strongly disagrees with the concept that biographical information is irrelevant to the understanding and evaluation of the poem. He is opposed to the point of view that deprives the poet of his right to explain his own poem or that challenges his claim to speak with final authority about his own work. He objects to the approach of the new critics that once the poem has been written, the author becomes just another reader. The concept that the author cannot protest against any interpretation if the poem is to be judged "successful" is, to Fiedler, absurd. Fiedler definitely does not object to the author discussing his "intentions" since, he feels, we can then judge the poem better. It is the bringing in from outside " . . . all kinds of rich relevancies and connecting them with the poem . . ." which makes it rich. Staying "inside the poem" will not permit this richness.[14]

According to Fiedler, the old biographists were unsuccessful because they failed to connect the facts with the work they presumed to illuminate. The proper use of biography, however, in conjunction with the work makes up the total meaning. It is this which will raise the meaning to a higher power.

Perhaps Fiedler's argument can be seen more clearly through an understanding of his definition of the poem, which he speaks of as Archetype and Signature. He defines Archetype as "any of the immemorial patterns of response to the human situation in its most permanent aspects: death, love, biological family, relation with Unknown . . . ,"[15] Signature he defines as the " . . . sum total of individuating factors in a work, the Persona or Personality, through which the Archetype is rendered and which itself tends to become a subject as well as the means of the poem."[16] Literature, he feels, comes into existence at the moment a Signature is imposed upon the Archetype. Without the Signature, there is only a myth.

[14]Fiedler, op. cit., pp. 257-259.

[15]Ibid., pp. 261-262.

[16]Ibid., p. 262.

- 6 -

Fiedler admonishes his reader to connect the "poet and the poem, the lived and the made, the Signature and the Archetype. It is on the focus of the poetic personality," he states, "that Dichtung [poetry] and Wahreit [sic, truth] become one; and it is incumbent upon us, without surrendering our right to make useful distinctions, to seize the principle of that unity. 'Only connect!'" (273)

Most critics of today shy away from taking either extreme position; that is, that biographical information is entirely extrinsic and hence has little, if any, value in the understanding and/or evaluation of a poem; and that biographical information is necessary to the complete understanding of the literary work. Most of the critics that I have thus far read take more of a middle-of-the-road point of view; that is, they will admit that biographical information can have certain value. Perhaps this comes in reaction to the feelings, as expressed by W.M. Frohock in an essay in Strangers to This Ground and cited by Granville Hicks, that "textual criticism is now triumphant in most of the universities. Biography is irrelevant; social background is irrelevant; nothing matters but the work of literature, and this the student scrutinizes with the care and precision of a microbiologist examining a segment of tissue." ("Gestation" 62)

Wellek and Warren, even though Hicks feels that they practice textual criticism with austerity, believe that, if used with discrimination, there is use in biographical study for it may explain a great many allusions or even words in an author's work (68).[1] However, Wellek and Warren continue to state that whatever the importance of biography in these respects, "it seems dangerous to ascribe to it any specifically critical importance. No biographical evidence can change or influence critical evaluation" (68).

Wellek and Warren are not alone in their beliefs. David Daiches feels that it is often useful and sometimes valuable to use biography and the work as a help in interpreting each other. However, he, too, limits this usefulness to interpretation and not for assessment:

---

[1]Fiedler illustrates this by using Donne's line from "Love's Alchemie": "they are but Mummy possesst." He points out that knowing of Donne's intimate relationship with his mother gives the reader cause to interpret this line that "women once possessed, turn out to be substitutes for the Mother who is the real end of our desiring." (265–266)

- 7 -

One could take the biography of a writer, as illustrated by the external events of his life and such things as letters and other confessional documents, and construct out of these a theory of the writer's personality—his conflicts, frustrations, traumatic experiences, neuroses, or whatever they happened to be—and use this theory in order to illuminate each one of his works. Or one can work back and forth between the life and the work, illuminating each by the other, noting from the biography certain crises reflected in the works, and seeing from the way they are reflected in the works what their real biographical meaning was. This is often dangerous, if highly stimulating, theorizing, and its relation to critical evaluations, at most, very tenuous. (345)

Elizabeth Nitchie in The Criticism of Literature also expresses similar feelings. Although she feels, on one hand, that it is well for the critic to know the biography of the author for it will aid him in better understanding the work, on the other hand, she feels that interesting though this type may be, the biography may well color and affect our evaluation, for "no man's literary work should be judged by his life" (13–14).

Louise Rosenblatt in Literature as Exploration finds that it may at times be necessary to place the literary work in the context of the life of the personality of the author since this may ". . . confirm for us more definitely those things that we sense in his work" (137). Knowledge about the author's life, she feels, and the literary influences acting upon him ". . . will create the need for understanding the intellectual and philosophical, the social and economic, conditions surrounding them" (138).

Perhaps part of this problem can be solved by differentiating between appreciation and/or understanding and criticism. Knowledge of the author's life may well help us in understanding and appreciating a work since without this biographical knowledge, elements in the poem may well elude us. Yet this knowledge will rarely if ever help us in evaluative criticism, in better seeing the work as it objectively is.

Even Tillyard sees the inherent danger in the mixture of biography and criticism. Although Tillyard finds that the danger may be in the reader using biography as an ". . . illegitimate short cut into the poet's mental pattern as revealed by his poems" (16), something akin to using a "crib when reading a foreign text" (16–17), I am more concerned with the reader arriving at an evaluation of the work which is based on nothing more than the author's intent or some biographical data which may have no bearing whatsoever on the poem.

- 8 -

thing akin to using "a crib when reading a foreign text,"[26] I am more concerned with the reader arriving at an evaluation of the work which is based on nothing more than the author's intent or some biographical data which may have no bearing whatsoever on the poem.

Thus far, I have yet to find a forceful and valid argument for the use of biography as an important factor in the evaluation of a poem. Nor have I found anything which will convince me that biographical knowledge prior to the reading of a poem is useful. Insofar as I am concerned, I share Professor Tillyard's fears that the student may use this as a short cut, but I fear it for different reasons. I am afraid that the student will "read into" the work things which are not there, things which he will not be able to substantiate from his reading of the poem.

Basic understanding and appreciation should be derived from the literary work itself, without the reader's awareness of the author's intent, for, first, the work must exist on its merits. Afterwards, perhaps, knowledge of the author's biography may prove useful in that it may shed further light on the reading and aid in greater understanding and appreciation. To this extent I will agree with Granville Hicks: "To isolate the literary object is a valid method of attack, but to leave it in isolation is a mistake"; " . . . anything that increases awareness is good."[27]

---

[26]Ibid., pp. 16–17.

[27]Hicks, loc. cit.

BIBLIOGRAPHY

Daiches, David. Critical Approaches to Literature. Englewood Cliffs, New Jersey: Prentice-Hall, Inc., 1956.

Fiedler, Leslie A. "Archetype and Signature: A Study of the Relationship between Biography and Poetry," Sewanee Review, 60:253-273. 1952.

Fishman, Solomon. The Disinherited of Art, Writer and Background. Los Angeles University of California Press, 1953.

Harris, Frank. The Man Shakespeare and His Tragic Life-Story. New York: Mitchell Kennerley, 1909.

Hicks, Granville. "Literary Horizons: Gestation of a Brain Child," Saturday Review, 45:62. January 6, 1962.

—————— . "Literary Horizons: The Newest Pamphleteers," Saturday Review, 44:23. November 11, 1961.

Lewis, C.S. "The Personal Heresy in Criticism," Essays and Studies by Members of the English Association. Collected by D. Nichol Smith. Oxford: The Clarendon Press, 1934. Vol. XIX, pp. 7-28.

Nitchie, Elizabeth. The Criticism of Literature. New York: The Macmillan Company, 1929.

Rosenblatt, Louise M. Literature as Exploration. New York: D. Appleton-Century Company, 1938.

Tillyard, E.M.W. "The Personal Heresy in Criticism, A Rejoinder," Essays and Studies by Members of the English Association. Collected by George Cookson. Oxford: The Clarendon Press, 1935. Vol. XX, pp. 7-20.

Wellek, Rene and Austin Warren. Theory of Literature. New York: Harcourt, Brace, and World, Inc., 1942. Chap. 7.

[SAMPLE]

TABLE OF CONTENTS

[SAMPLE]

LIST OF TABLES

APPENDIX II

ABBREVIATIONS AND SYMBOLS USED IN FOOTNOTES AND BIBLIOGRAPHIES

anon.	anonymous
art., arts.	article(s)
bk., bks.	book(s)
c.	copyright
c., ca.	*circa* (about; approximately)
cf.	*confer* (compare)
ch., chap., chs., chaps.	chapter(s)
col., cols.	column(s)
diss.	dissertation
ed., edn.	edition
ed., eds.	editor(s); when preceding the name, it means "edited by"
e.g.	*exempli gratia* (for example)
esp.	especially
et al.	*et alii* (and others)
f., ff.	the following page(s), e.g., p.11f. or p. 11ff.
ibid.	*ibidem* (in the same place)
i.e.	*id est* (that is)
introd.	introduction
l., ll.	line(s)
loc. cit.	*loco citato* (in the place cited)
MS, MSS, ms., mss.	manuscript(s)
N.B., n.b.	*nota bene* (take notice)
n.d.	no date given
n.p.	no publisher or place of publication given
No., Nos.	number(s)
numb.	numbered
op. cit.	*opere citato* (in the work cited)
p., pp.	page(s)

passim	here and there
par., pars.	paragraph(s)
rev.	revised
sic	thus
tr., trns., trans.	translator, translated, translation
v.	*vide* (see)
vs., vss.	verse(s)
vol., vols.	volume(s)
...	ellipsis
/	line division in short verse quotations when not set off from text
[ ]	inclusion of editorial material within quotation